MASTERING
COLLEGE
TO CAREER

DANIEL BOTERO

DEDICATION

I would like to dedicate this book to the following people:

My Mother

When I think about what I've accomplished in my life thus far, I know that it wouldn't have been possible without your sacrifice. I know that if you would have never made the decision to move to the U.S. and work 7 days a week for over 15 years, that I would not have had the opportunity to graduate college in 4 years with 2 majors, work for a Fortune 500 company managing over $100 million dollars in yearly sales, build a new house at the age of 23, and write this book. These accomplishments would not have been possible without you. This is why I'm eternally grateful and I don't think that I'll ever be able to repay you. I want you to know that we are a team and what I accomplish is not just my accomplishment, but it's your accomplishment too. Thank you for your unconditional love and support. I love you mom!

My Wife

Thank you for all of the support that you've given me throughout our relationship, especially in this last year. You've supported me by allowing me to follow my dream and work full time on the Mastering College to Career business. You've supported me mentally when I've felt down or anxious. You've supported me financially as you continue to work in your corporate job. And last but not least, you've supported me in writing this book by spending countless hours editing. You've supported me every step of the way and I can always count on you to give me clarity when I really need it. I hope you know that there is no way that this book would have become a reality if it wasn't for you. This book is just as much yours as it is mine. I truly believe that if it wasn't for you, my goals wouldn't have been possible. Thank you for being the best wife, the best friend, and the best business partner there is. I love you Jessica Botero! I said it on our wedding day and I will say it again.. you are my biggest accomplishment.

GET YOUR FREE MINI COURSE HERE!

To say thank you AGAIN. I've also created a mini course that I would like to give you for **FREE.**

Or visit http://bit.ly/mc2cminicourse

TABLE OF CONTENTS

INTRODUCTION TO MASTERING
COLLEGE TO CAREER

CHAPTER 1
WHY MC2C SHOULD BE YOUR #1 PRIORITY

Understanding The Facts

If we met in high school and I told you that you should spend the next six years of your life attending college and racking up $30,000 in student loan debt only to graduate without a job, what would you tell me?

You would probably tell me I'm crazy because that sounds like a terrible investment of time and money and I agree! Unfortunately, this happens to a lot of people.

Here are the facts!

- 67% of college students graduate without a job lined up*

- 40% of graduates are in jobs that don't require a degree**

- The average college student is taking six years to graduate with a four-year degree***

- On average students are graduating with $30,000 in student debt****

These numbers sound really bad as it is, but the reality is that these numbers get even worse when you look at first-generation college students and minorities.

Student Story

Let me tell you a story of two students, Danielle and Mike.

Danielle is an individual I met in middle school. Yes, middle school! Throughout the years we would run into each other every once in a while and say hi, but that was the extent of our friendship. About two years ago she contacted me after years of not speaking. She said, "Hi Daniel, I hope you are doing well. I wanted to reach out because I know that you help college students get a job after graduation. I graduate in a couple of months and I would love to see if you can help me. About a year ago you helped a mutual friend of ours get a great job and I thought you could help me do the same." I replied to her message and agreed to talk to her about it.

A week later, Danielle and I jumped on a call. I still remember the phone call like it was yesterday. I was in Atlanta for work and I had just finished a meeting with Target when I decided to take her call in the car. Danielle started the call by telling me how grateful she was that I made time to speak to her. We spoke for about an hour and I remember getting off the phone feeling like I had to help her. At that time, Danielle had been working for Olive Garden for ten years as a server. She was working full time, taking care of her two young daughters, and finishing her degree.

Now I'll tell you the story of Mike. Mike was a student I met in the fall of 2017 when I was judging final presentations for one of the professors with whom I have a great relationship. In this scenario, the professor asked me if I had time after class to talk. He asked if I had remembered Mike from group three. I told him that I did and that he did a great job speaking on his part. The professor went on to share that he has been keeping a close eye on Mike all semester and that he's concerned because Mike lacks the confidence needed to land a job after college. He went on to share that Mike was the first in his family to attend college and that he had been working at a pizza shop for the past four years while he finished his business degree. He then shared that Mike would graduate in two weeks, and asked if I could meet with Mike to try and help him find a job. I told the professor to feel free to share my information with Mike and that I would help him as much as he would allow.

I could go on and on sharing stories of students just like Danielle and Mike. The reality is that the stories may be different, but the results generally end up being the same. Students all over the U.S. are graduating without a job, and that is a fact. Remember, 67% of students are walking across the graduation stage with no job lined up. Danielle and Mike are no different; at the end of the book, I share with you what happened with those two students.

I have asked thousands of students why they decided to attend college and I've heard every reason you can imagine. Most students say it's to make more money or because their parents told them they had to or because they want a good career. These are all good reasons, but ultimately it all comes down to one reason. People attend college because they believe that they will have better opportunities than they would by not attending college.

There are not many places that give you the level of opportunity that college provides if you fully take advantage of it. By reading this book you will learn how to take full advantage of what college has to offer and ultimately Master College and land your dream job.

Income Inequality

Your first job after college is more important than most people think. It creates a foundation for the rest of your professional life. After your first job you will not be judged based on what you accomplished in college, but rather on what you have done after college. If you take a job in which you are making $30,000 a year, it will be almost impossible for you to make a big jump to making $60,000 a year quickly. At the end of the day, your value is determined by the market. The great thing about college is that you have the ability to make a difference in your income potential. I want to ensure that you make the right job selection out of college, otherwise, it will be difficult to rise above that low starting base.

Let's look at an example of two students. One student landed a job making $30,000 per year and the second student landed a job making $60,000 per year. Both graduated with the same major and attended the same school. The student making $60,000 did not put in double the effort, but instead had a clear plan. He knew which jobs paid more and he knew what he needed to do to land those jobs. Take a look at the graph below. In year one, the difference in income between the two students is $30,000. If each student receives a 5% annual increase, the difference in income will be $80,000 by year twenty. Most college students are not thinking about twenty years after graduation, but as you can see, the choices we make in college affect us for the rest of our lives. It is important that you take this book seriously because this book will give you the tools you need to land those great job opportunities that will make a world of difference for the rest of your life.

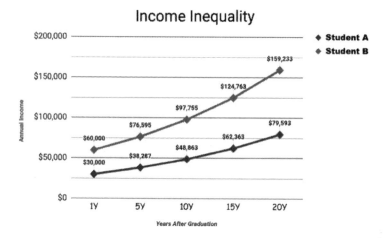

Income Inequality

Annual Income

$200,000
$159,233
$150,000
$124,763
$97,755
$100,000
$76,595
$79,593
$60,000
$62,363
$48,863
$50,000
$38,287
$30,000
$0

1Y   5Y   10Y   15Y   20Y

Years After Graduation

◆ Student A
◆ Student B

A Very Common Scenario

Earlier in the book, I gave you those daunting statistics and shared that 67% of students walk across the graduation stage without a job lined up. I also shared that 40% of graduates are in jobs that don't require a degree. I don't know about you, but when I first heard those statistics I was shocked and I did not believe them. I want you to think about two things. The first thing I want you to think about is if you know anyone who is part of those statistics? Really think about who those people might be. The chances are that you know multiple people who fit in that group. They may not be open to sharing their life because let's be honest, who wants to share that they attended college, could not find a job, and now are working in a job that they could have done without college? The second thing I want you to really think about is, am I on track to get caught in that same trap? The reality is that this is not something that happens overnight. Graduating without a job is a result of what you did during college, not what you did the day after you walked across the stage to accept your diploma.

Let's look at a common scenario I see happen way too often. You are a senior in college and this is your last semester. You have been in college for almost six years and you can't wait to graduate. The past six years have been fun, but you can't wait to be done. This has taken so much longer than expected. Like many of your friends, you changed your major as a junior, after getting into your higher level classes because you realized that you did not enjoy it as much as you thought you would. You needed some extra money while in college so you picked up a job as a hostess. You have been working at this restaurant the entire time that you've been in college. You are now a server and since you have been there for quite a while you have seniority which means you get to choose your days off and pick the good sections allowing you to make good money as a college student. Working throughout college has provided you with a good income, but you were not able to get as involved as you really wanted to in other activities that your school provided. Between working full time, being a full-time student, and hanging out with friends, you are very busy. For the past six years, you have not made finding a job a priority. You thought that with your solid work experience, doing an internship your junior year, and the fact that your managers say you have management potential, that you would have no problem finding a job after graduation. I mean, the unemployment rate is at an all-time low after all!

The semester flew by and you got really busy with studying. You knew that you had to focus on school because failing any of your classes means you would need to retake them and that would delay your graduation. So for the meantime, you focus on your school work and job. Time flies and you find yourself walking across the stage at graduation without a job lined up. This was a very special day. You had all of your family and friends celebrating your accomplishment. You can't believe it! All those years of hard work paid off. You are now a college graduate! You are ready to take on

8

the world.

A couple of days after graduation everything starts sinking in. It feels weird now that you don't have classes to worry about. You then try to figure out what your next move should be. Getting your degree is great and all, but you need to find a job. You sit down and you start researching jobs. You are motivated and set a goal of applying to fifty jobs each week. With more time on your hands, you start working five nights at the restaurant. You tell yourself that you will keep serving until you get a job using your degree because at the end of the day you have bills to pay.

Weeks go by and you are starting to stress out. You are not getting any traction. You spent the first couple of weeks applying to all of the big companies that pay well and have a lot of room for growth. You applied to hundreds of companies and roles but only heard back from two. You interviewed with those companies but you have not heard back since the interviews. You find out that you don't have the skills bigger companies are looking for so you focus on smaller businesses. At this point, you are really stressing out. You worked so hard to get a degree and now you can't find a job. Then you receive an email letting you know that you will need to start paying your $30,000 worth of student loan debt starting in a couple of months.

A couple of months go by and you finally receive a call from a company with a job offer. The job offer you receive has nothing to do with your degree. Everyone in the office really liked you and they were in need of a new office manager. At first, you are ecstatic about having a job offer, but then you start thinking about how you will be taking a major pay cut and how this job does not require your degree. You make $48,000 a year as a server and your current offer for this position is $30,000 a year. You have a critical decision to make that will impact you for the rest of your life. So, you go through your options.

Option A: You take the job. It's not your ideal job, but at least it will get your foot in the door. You will be able to work your way up, or worst-case scenario, you can gain experience and use this job as a stepping stone for future opportunities. You would need to continue working at the restaurant part-time to make enough money to continue living the life you're accustomed to. It is human nature to have our expenses match our income and this student is no exception.

Option B: You can decline the job offer and keep looking. You can always continue working at the restaurant while applying and interviewing for jobs on your days off.

Regardless of what option you decide to take, you feel like your back is against the wall. It seems that with every minute that goes by where you're not working at a job related to your degree, the harder it is for you to find a job. Companies see that as a red flag. Why did you not start looking earlier? Why did you not have a job lined up before graduation? If you took that long to take your career seriously, then why would I want to hire you? I have personally worked for companies that would not hire people for their college program if they graduated more than a year ago. This definitely limits your options.

I see the above scenario happen all of the time. This is why it felt so real, as if I was describing a real person. When people reach out to me for help after being out of school for months my heart breaks. The reality is that it's ten-times harder to find a job that they're looking for at that point. I'm sharing this scenario because I don't want this to happen to you!

I challenge you to make mastering your journey from college to career your number one priority. Landing your dream job was the goal you had when you came to college in the first place. By deciding to make this your priority you will completely change the outcome of your life. Give yourself a pat on the back for picking up this book and finishing the first chapter. I promise that if you apply what you learn from this book you will Master College and land your dream job before graduation.

CHAPTER 2
WHY ME

My College Story

The reality is that I should have been one of the students to make up those statistics that I just gave you. I was a first-generation college student and I'm a minority.

I remember graduating high school desiring to go to college, but not knowing how to navigate the system. I was going to be a first-generation college student and I had no idea what I was doing. I had no clue that I needed to study for the SAT my sophomore and junior year of high school. I did not apply to any universities because I knew I wouldn't get in. I remember going to my local community college with a folder full of papers to turn in to the advisor which included everything I could think of, such as my mom's utility bill, tax returns, high school transcript, and my resume. I was so scared and I wondered how I was going to be able to register or figure out which classes to choose. I had no guidance outside of the people who worked at the help desk. I remember walking into the office waiting to speak to an advisor who was going to help me choose the classes I would take to get my A.A. and transfer to a state university. I was lucky enough that I always knew what I wanted to do when I grew up, but I had no idea how to get there.

I'm going to be honest. When I was a college student I was naive and I didn't know that graduating college without a job was even an option. I just assumed that if I attended a university in the U.S., I would be guaranteed a job and be able to live the American dream.

I always assumed that college was the gateway to the American dream.

My college career started at Valencia College. I spent my first couple of semesters taking English and Math courses to bring me to college level. I was so ashamed that I didn't tell anyone. From the beginning, I was behind schedule, but I didn't let that stop me. I was focused on getting my A.A. in two years and receiving my bachelor's degree in four years.

One thing that helped me is that I always knew I wanted to get my bachelors degree in business. Business always interested me and I knew that I wanted to start my own business and make a lot of money. That level of clarity gave me a HUGE advantage. Though, I didn't realize how big of an advantage it was until after graduation. While at Community College, I completed my first internship. Again, because of my level of clarity I knew the internship would be very important. I remember searching and applying for internships and not having much luck. I felt the same level of frustration we all have with rejection. I wanted to do an internship to get work experience, but those opportunities require experience. I finally found someone who gave me my first internship. His name was Joe Durek and he was the CEO of Protostar International. Joe didn't have any employees working for him so It was just Joe and I working from his home office. He gave me a shot and took me under his wing. I still remember going home and telling my mom about acquiring my first internship. I thought she would be so happy for me, but instead, she had a confused look on her face and actually got mad at me. I remember her words like it was yesterday. She told me I was an idiot because I was working for free, while my friends were working as servers making good money. She told me that I was getting taken advantage of because I was an immigrant. She couldn't understand why I would work forty hours a week for free. I told her that I needed to sacrifice my time now to be able to make money in the future. I don't blame her for thinking and saying those things, but this unpaid internship taught me so much. It really opened my eyes to business and the possibilities that having your own business can bring.

Fast forward to two years later and I received my Associates of Arts degree from Valencia and I used their Direct Connect Program to be admitted to the University of Central Florida (UCF). At this point, I was on track to achieve my goals with an A.A. degree and an internship under my belt. During my first semester at UCF, I took all of the business core classes. I knew that I was interested in business, but didn't know which major within the business college I wanted to pursue. In my second semester, I made a life-changing decision to rush for Delta Sigma Pi, a professional business fraternity. This decision impacted my life immensely for many reasons. I was surrounded with like-minded individuals and I was able to learn from students who already had jobs lined up before graduation. I also found purpose in college outside of just going to class. Joining this organization taught me the importance of networking and how working together as a group opens up so many doors. I saw how my brothers who were graduating were passing down their college internships to younger brothers. I also no longer had to buy textbooks because they were traded and shared between the brothers.

While at UCF I completed three more internships. Those internships included: Tutoring Matching Service, Revenue Performance, and Enterprise Rent-A-Car. I also worked part-time at Universal Studios and Publix Super Market. In addition to gaining valuable work experience with internships, I also got the chance to learn what I enjoyed and didn't care for in work, school, and life. I didn't really realize this at the time but these experiences were so important in my college-to-career journey. Those internships allowed me to gain clarity in identifying my strengths and weaknesses. For example, my internship as an account manager for Revenue Performance was my least favorite job. It wasn't because it was a bad company, but my assigned tasks didn't play into my strengths and I therefore didn't enjoy what I was doing.

To me, everything I did while I was in college helped me figure out what I wanted to do with my life. I figured out what I really disliked and what I liked and needed to explore more. Everything that I did got me one step closer to my long term goals.

Going into my senior year I was still indecisive. I knew that I wanted to major in management with a track of entrepreneurship, but I also wanted to be part of the professional selling program. At this time in my life, I was listening to one audiobook each week. Based on everything that I had learned in these audio books, I realized that I needed to have experience in two areas to run my own successful business one day. I needed to be good at sales because nothing happens until something is sold. I also needed to be good at management because you can't scale a business alone. I came to the conclusion that I could hire someone else to do the other parts of the business and that I would focus my efforts on sales and management.

Since I couldn't decide on one major, I double-majored in management with a track of entrepreneurship, and marketing with a professional selling track.

I got accepted into UCF's professional selling program. This is a very prestigious sales program, and is ranked as one of the best in the country. Only thirty students are accepted each year and I was ecstatic to be one of them. This program was also life-changing for me. Being part of this program opened a lot of doors to different companies. The program has corporate partners that pay money to the school to be front and center to those thirty students. Companies were paying thousands of dollars each year to be able to recruit us.

This was when options began to appear for me. I had companies reach out to me just because I was part of this program.

In addition to being part of this program, I had networked and built a relationship with the career services department. I will dive into how crucial and helpful this relationship was in a later chapter.

Fast forward to the end of my college career and I was graduating from the University of Central Florida with a double major in management and marketing. Best of all, I had a job lined up with my dream company! In fact, I was being recruited like a five-star-athlete and had multiple job offers to choose from.

I even had a company tell me to look at their website and pick three cities that I could see myself living in. They told me they would fly me to all three cities to spend a day in their local offices and have activities planned for me on the weekend. I was like, *"heck yes, three free trips!"* Ultimately I chose not to take them up on their offer. My professor asked me to respectfully decline it if I was not fully committed to the company because it would give UCF a bad name and it would hurt the chances for future students to have this awesome opportunity.

After a lot of research, interviews, and thinking about my future, I accepted a job with Frito Lay, a Division of PepsiCo and a Fortune 50 company. I was hired for their management training program. In this role, I started as a sales associate and after a year of training, I could be promoted to district sales manager.

I chose Frito Lay because it was a unique opportunity to manage a team and work in sales. This allowed me to use what I learned from both of my majors right away. All of my other job offers were either going to be focused on selling or focused on management, but not both. The opportunity to manage a sales team and, essentially, run a multi-million dollar business with the backing of a Fortune 50 company was ideal for both my short term and long term goals. Plus, the pay was great too! I was making almost double the average college student.

During my time with Frito Lay, I was part of the college campus hiring team. After two years, I became the team captain for my alma mater UCF. I was so involved at UCF and I recruited so many UCF students that I was able to get our Vice President of Human Resources to help make UCF a core recruiting school for all of PepsiCo. This means that the university would receive additional resources from PepsiCo headquarters and that a majority of college hires for PepsiCo's college program would come from those core schools. Because of this, UCF students had a better opportunity to get a job with Pepsico than non-core schools.

My Transition From Corporate America To Helping Students Master College

Being part of the campus hiring team was where I found my passion for helping college students land their dream job. I was able to see things from a different perspective because I was now on the other side of the table.

After I completed my training and became a district sales manager, I attended my first career expo as an employer. It was an eye-opening experience. I never realized that I was the exception in college when it came to being prepared for graduation. Maybe it was because I was naive and thought everyone who attended college in the U.S. would automatically receive a job or maybe it was because the people whom I surrounded myself with also had great opportunities, but regardless it was an awakening moment. I came to realize that not everyone has a clear approach to job searching and that not everyone has options as I did.

18

I continued to be involved with the campus hires, and I was also invited to speak about Frito Lay and PepsiCo by the same student organizations that I was involved in and even by my old professors.

This is how my speaking started; by speaking about my personal experiences and the job opportunities that PepsiCo had to offer. Even in that first year, I was speaking about five times per semester. I was so intrigued with understanding what the students who received jobs before graduation had in common and what set them apart from other students. I read every book that I could find on the topic. Between reading, speaking with professors, and my personal success story I started to formulate a program that students could use to guarantee them a job before they graduated. At this point in time, my friends from high school were getting ready to graduate. Keep in mind that I graduated in four years, but the average student takes six years. Many of my friends saw that I had gotten a really good job and reached out to me for help. The first students I helped were my high school friends. Because I only knew Pepsico, in my first two years of helping students I only helped students who were interested in working at PepsiCo. I helped them become the ideal candidate. In fact, I helped over a dozen UCF students get a job with PepsiCo. At that time, PepsiCo gave me a $1,500 referral bonus for every person I brought in and they hired. My boss often joked that I made more money from my referral bonus than my yearly bonus. Which I did.

As time passed, I started testing my program with students who didn't want to work for PepsiCo, but rather with other companies too. As word of my speaking and success in helping others started spreading, I was invited to speak at other universities.

Fast forward to five years later and I had helped hundreds of students land their dream job. I had spoken in front of students from over eight different colleges and universities, and I felt that I found my calling.

At this time I was torn with what to do next in my career. I loved working at Frito Lay. They were really good to me and I was even up for a promotion. My other option was to focus on building my speaking business and help even more students. I had been going back and forth with what to do next and at the same time, I was in the middle of the interview process for a promotion. I remember talking to my wife and asking her if she would support me leaving Frito Lay to follow my passion. That same day my wife said she would support my decision, I received a call from my boss. She called to let me know that out of the thirty people who applied for the role, I was one of the final two chosen. All I had to do was to interview with the vice president. When I heard the news I felt even more torn, and I think my boss sensed something was wrong. Ten minutes after she called me to share the good news, I called her back and gave her my two-week notice.

That had to be one of the hardest decisions of my life. It was something that I had to do to make my passion into my business. I did not start Mastering College To Career right away, but instead, I went into staffing. I worked in staffing for about six months and learned a lot about the industry and talent acquisition. That experience allowed me to really understand other companies, and other industries hiring needs.

Long story short, the combination of my personal experience in college, understanding how college hiring for a Fortune 50 company works, countless hours worth of research on this topic, understanding first hand the challenges students face, speaking in front of thousands of students from over thirty universities, interviewing industry experts for my podcast, and personally testing my theory with hundreds of students who have successfully landed their dream job using my approach is why you should listen to me. I am so confident that this will work for you that I have risked my professional career on this. I left a six-figure corporate job and the lucrative staffing industry all to focus 100% on making the Mastering College To Career business a success and be able to reach my goal of helping one million students take away their fear of graduating without a job and instead teach them how to land their dream job!

CHAPTER 3
THE GOAL

Why Read This Book

Like I mentioned at the end of the last chapter, I wrote this book because my goal is to help one million students take away their fear of graduating without a job and instead teach them how to land their dream job. Over the past five years I have personally helped hundreds of students do just that. In fact, every student I've worked with on a one-on-one basis has received at least one job offer. I have read every book written on helping students transition from college to career and they all fail to do one thing. They fail to make the content relevant to college students. What I've found is that most of these books were written by either professors who have spent their whole life in academia not fully understanding the recruiting process from a company's point of view, or by successful business people who are disconnected from the obstacles that college students face today. Don't get me wrong, those books are useful and I will actually cover some similar material in this book. Since those authors have either never had to search for a job themselves or they're too disconnected to really understand the pain-points that college students face today, this book fills in the gap. I have read all of these books and I have interviewed hundreds of industry experts such as CEO's, company presidents, HR Directors, university presidents, directors of employee relations at universities, professors, recruiters, individuals in charge of college campus programs for billion-dollar organizations, deans of colleges, and best of all, hundreds of students. Using the knowledge that I've gained through my five-plus years of campus hiring for a Fortune 50 company and mentoring over a hundred students to help them land their dream job, I created a proprietary program that I will cover step-by-step in this book.

This book is broken down into five sections:

1. Introduction

2. Assess

3. Acquire

4. Achieve

5. Conclusion

The meat and potatoes of the book are in the three middle sections: Assess, Acquire, and Achieve. I call those sections the 3 A's. My program revolves around the 3 A's, which I will explain in the next few chapters.

Assess

The first step of the three-step program is to Assess. Like constructing a tall building, the foundation is crucial for the success of the project. We can't build the second or third floor without making sure we have laid a solid foundation. If we do, the building will likely collapse. This is why Assess is the first step of the program. In this section, the goal is to help you complete a self-assessment. Taking the time to do a thorough self-assessment will save you money, time, and energy in the long run. It will help you avoid picking the wrong major, or even worse, choosing a job right out of college that does not help you get closer to your long term goals. I have seen this happen way too often so please make sure you take this section seriously. Warning! Self-awareness can come easy to some, but for the majority of students, this is difficult. Don't be discouraged if you're having trouble figuring out what you want to do after college. If you work hard at figuring it out it will come to you.

This section is divided into three chapters. The first chapter will focus on making sure that you understand the importance of conducting self-assessments. In the second chapter, we will go through my Mastering College To Career Assessment Workbook. It will help you gain clarity about your future and it will help you start creating your college roadmap. In the last chapter, we will talk about how landing your dream job is an open book test and I'll share with you how to find those answers. By the time you are done with this section of the book, you will have done a self-assessment, built your target list of companies, and figured out the answers to your open book test. After all of that, it will be time to move on to the next section of the book: Acquire!

Acquire

By the time you get to this section, you will be focusing on acquiring the skills that your target companies are looking for and preparing yourself to be their ideal candidate. We will also cover important topics such as why networking is king, how to be strategic with your time, why you should run yourself like a business, and I'll show you how to take advantage of the fact that you are a student. In this section, I really dive into strategy. We'll be focusing on the things that are going to make you stand out among your peers and make recruiters so impressed that they'll be reaching out to you. This section is unconventional and it's what makes my book so different from other books or articles on this topic. By the time you finish this section, you will have a road map for your college career and you will know exactly how to stand out. You will be recruited like a five-star-athlete.

Achieve

In the Achieve section, we will focus on the final touches of your master plan. I am going to teach you how to stand out among your peers. This can be difficult since we spend our whole life trying to fit in, and now I'm telling you that you need to stand out. We will also go over how to properly approach the employers and how to start building a relationship with the talent acquisition/human resources team. We will then talk about your resume. I will not tell you how to write a resume. You can get that advice for free from your career services department. Instead, I will show you how to ensure that you are handing your resume to the right person. Everything you have learned thus far will help you stand out and help you get an interview, but it doesn't matter unless you are able to close the sale. What I mean by closing the sale is receiving the job offer and landing your dream job before graduation. This is why, in this section, we dive into landing the interview, nailing the interview, and the best way to follow up after the interview.

The 3 A's Will Work For All Students

Regardless if you are a freshman or a senior in college, you will see that the 3 A's program will work for you. Obviously, the more time you have to implement the program, the better it will work and the more opportunities you will have, but regardless, this system can be adjusted to work for a senior.

The reason that this will work regardless of where you are in your college career is that this proprietary program helps you to focus and create a plan for success. Proper planning prevents poor performance and focusing your attention on three to five companies will always be better than casting a wide net.

As a freshman, you have the advantage of time. You have four years to narrow your options. This is a huge advantage if you can realize it and not take it for granted. Many times, freshmen think that they have all the time in the world. They start justifying why they can wait until next semester to start, but in the blink of an eye they too become seniors and time is now their biggest enemy. Don't be this person! Time goes by way too quick and college will be over before you know it.

As a senior, you don't have time on your side. The same thing occurs when you decide to wait until the last minute to study for an exam. You double your efforts and make sure you're focusing on the task at hand. This is where, you as a senior, have an advantage. You know that time is running out and you are faster at taking action. Also, by this time in your college career, you have more experience which will allow you to take shortcuts with your self-assessment. This will save you time, but it is a reactive approach versus the proactive approach a freshman can take.

In the end, if you apply the 3 A's (Assess, Acquire, and Achieve) you will have a job lined up before graduation.

ASSESS

CHAPTER 4
THE IMPORTANCE OF ASSESS

Everyone Get Up!

When I am giving my signature talk in front of students, I always start with an activity. I want to show students that if they are feeling lost and confused about what they want their future to look like, that it's okay. Most people feel that way. To start the activity I have everyone stand up. Then I say, "anyone who has ever changed their major, please sit down." Over half of the room sits down everytime. Next, I tell them that if they have ever taken a class that did not count toward their major to please sit down. By this time, I have about 80% of the students sitting down. Then I tell them that if they have no idea what they want to do after graduation to please sit down. At least 90% of the students are sitting down at this point. I have done this activity for the past two years and the results are always the same. This activity illustrates a couple of things. The number one thing that I want students to take away from this activity is that they are not alone. A lot of people struggle trying to figure out what they want to do with their life. The second thing I want them to realize is that they have already wasted thousands of dollars and hundreds of hours of their time. Think about it. Let's say that the average student takes four classes that do not count toward their major. For simple math, it costs about $1000 per class. You have not only spent $4,000 more than you should have, but you also spent the time attending the class, studying for the class, and everything else that goes with taking a class. This does not even take into account the opportunity cost for whatever else you could have done with that time.

The reality is that over 80% of college students change their major. By changing your major, you will likely need to take additional classes which adds more time spent in college. This is why it is now taking the average student six years to graduate with a four-year degree.

As you can see, it's important for you to take the time NOW to do self-assessments and to figure out what your dream job is after graduation. I think it's best to figure out what your goals and aspirations are first and then work backwards to create a plan to get there. Your goals and aspirations should help determine your dream career, dream job, major, and so on.

Student Story

I'm going to tell you a story about Tony, a student who went through my mentoring program. Like every student that I work with we always start with their self-assessment. I have every student fill out the MC2C Assessment Workbook. In this workbook, which you will complete later in this book, I had Tony create a target list. A target list is a list of the top ten companies you can see yourself working for. In this portion of the workbook, I have the students narrow their focus and become experts in those ten companies. The goal is to continue to narrow the target list until you've chosen your top five companies.

In this specific scenario, I met with Tony to review his MC2C Workbook at a coffee shop. Tony handed me his workbook and as I scanned through I noticed that Tony only had one company on his target list. I said, "Tony why do you only have one name on your target list? You should have at least five." Tony replied, "I don't need to have that many companies on my list because I already know where I want to work. One of my good friends works for that company and he loves it. I can totally see myself working there." I replied back, "Tony, what do you love about that company? How much research have you actually done on it? Have you ever spent time job shadowing your friend to see what a day or week would look like? Just because it is the right company for your friend does not mean that it's the right fit for you. Based on your answers in the earlier portion of the workbook, this company does not seem to match what you're looking for. Why don't you take a week to research the company and try to connect with ten people who work there and see what they like the most and what they like the least? Let's start this conversation again next week. Your first job out of college is very important and it sets the foundation for your professional career. If you can't see yourself working for them for two years, then this is not the right company." Tony told me that he would do what I suggested.

About two weeks later, Tony came back to me with a brand new workbook completed. He said to me, "Daniel, I took your advice and I went back and re-did your workbook and did more research on the company that I had selected. You were right that this is not the right company for me. It does not align with my long-term goals. I was so set on working for them that I was not taking the right amount of time to do my homework to figure out that I would have been miserable working there. Thank you so much! I'm not sure what would have happened if you didn't challenge me to take the time to do a complete self-assessment."

Tony is not alone on this. This happens to almost every student. We think that we would really love something only to find out that it's not a good fit at all. The only difference with Tony is that he was able to figure this out early on and he learned the importance of self-assessment.

One of the biggest mistakes that college students make is that they don't take the time to do these self-assessments. They are making important decisions based on how they feel on that specific day. They are not thinking about how the decisions that they make while in college will impact them for the rest of their lives.

100 MPH In The Wrong Direction

Think about this. Do you spend more time planning your vacations or do you spend more time planning your life after college? Be honest with yourself and let that sink in. The reality is that the majority of students plan their vacations really well. They have places they want to visit, they find a way to save the money, they look up reviews, and they see what the best places to eat and stay are. Now, what if you did that with your career? How would your career be different?

One thing that I see with college students is that they are always going 100 m.p.h. They seem to always be so busy and in a rush. Who will get to their destination faster? A student going 100 m.p.h. in the wrong direction or a student going 10 m.p.h. in the right direction?

I challenge you to be different and to realize that the most important thing that you can do now is to take the time to do a self-assessment. Throughout the rest of the Assess portion of the book, I will ask you important questions and give you the tools that will help you figure out your end goal. This will save you time and money in the long run. When you get to this part of the workbook, I don't want you to read it and say, "I will come back to it later." I want you to take action and complete the activities. This book is not meant for you to just read and put away. You should read the book, complete all of the activities in the workbook, and then reread the book as needed throughout your college-to-career journey.

CHAPTER 5
SELF DISCOVERY

Self-Assessment

We have talked about why conducting a self-assessment is important so now it's time to do it! I want you to take your time while completing this short assessment. This is intended to help you create a path for yourself.

You want to start by getting an idea of what your dream job will look like. In my experience, I have found that your dream job will lie somewhere between what you are passionate about and what you are naturally good at. Here is what I mean by that. I love basketball, but no matter how much milk I drank as a kid I did not grow much taller than 5'9". The reality is that I'm just not tall enough or good enough to make it to the NBA, no matter how much I love it. This is why I say that your dream job should be something that you are passionate about but also something that you are naturally good at.

So now it is your turn. I want you to list what you're passionate about on the left side of the venn diagram and what you're naturally good at on the right side. Once you've finished this, I want you to start thinking about jobs and careers that would utilize both your passions and your natural abilities.

SELF ASSESSMENT

Answer the questions below to get a better idea of where
your passions and strengths intersect.

What are you naturally good at?   What are you passionate about?

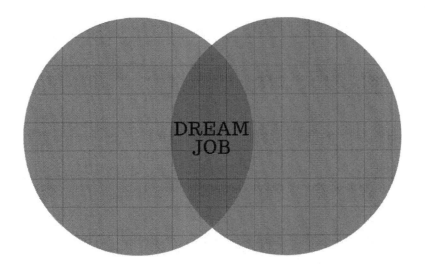

DREAM
JOB

What jobs encompass both what you're passionate
about and what you're naturally good at?

MasteringCollegeToCareer.Com

Establishing Your Life Vision

Now that you've filled out the above Venn diagram, it's time to reverse engineer your life. I want to force you to think five to ten years into the future. Start thinking about what your ideal life would look like. The more clear you are in understanding what your ideal life would like, the better you can plan for that life to actually make it a reality.

ESTABLISH YOUR LIFE VISION

Answer the questions below to gain clarity on what your ideal life would look like and figure out how you can make it happen.

If you made $150k regardless of your job, what career would you choose?

_____
_____
_____
_____
_____
_____

Where do you see your life 5-10 years from now?

_____
_____
_____
_____
_____
_____

Based on your responses to the last two questions, can you think backwards and figure out how you could get there in your career? Think of the steps that you would need to take in order to make your ideal life a reality.

_____
_____
_____
_____
_____
_____
_____
_____
_____

SWOT Analysis

A SWOT analysis is an analysis that you do when you are starting a new business or a new project. SWOT stands for Strengths, Weaknesses, Opportunities, and Threats. To complete this analysis, you start by dividing a piece of paper into four quadrants. You label each quadrant with each of the four words that make up SWOT. The top two quadrants should be "Strengths" and "Weaknesses". These are controlled by you. The bottom two quadrants, Opportunities and Threats, are out of your control. Business's use this analysis to understand what their competitive advantages are. They figure out what strengths they have that will allow them to win in the marketplace. They also try to understand their weaknesses in order to create plans to improve those weaknesses over time. Opportunities are things that are out of the companies control but will help the business. For example, an opportunity could be receiving low-interest rates or tax cuts from the government. Threats are the opposite of opportunities. Threats are things that are out of the companies control but can hurt the company. These may include things like the low unemployment rate or being in a trade war with a country you depend on for sales.

Similar to using the SWOT analysis for a business, I want you to apply it to yourself. I want you to identify your strengths. Are you a good leader? Do you have a photographic memory? Are you good at delegating? Are you good at writing? Write everything down that you can think of. Do the same with your weaknesses. Too often I see students struggling to write down their weaknesses. They think that it's a sign of weakness to write them down, but it's actually the opposite. Self-awareness is a major strength and the ability to see your strengths next to your weaknesses will allow you to think more clearly. If you write your weaknesses down and you don't want to share them with anyone that's okay. This is only for your benefit.

After you've finished listing your weaknesses, it's time to write down your opportunities. As a student, these will vary based on your major and the industry that you are trying to get into, but there are some that apply to all students. One opportunity that all students have currently is the low unemployment rate. This is something that all college graduates can benefit from because companies are in need of good talent. Now, let's move onto threats. Threats for college students again will vary by the major, industry, and company that you're looking to get into. One threat that can affect students is the fact that we have been in a growing market for over ten years and experts predict a downturn in the near future. When this happens companies tend to play defensively and invest less in hiring. This is just an example, but you will need to research to figure out your personal threats.

It is now your turn to conduct your personal SWOT analysis.

SWOT ANALYSIS

Write down your strengths and weaknesses below. These are things that you have control of and can change. Next, write down your opportunities and threats. These are factors that affect you but are out of your control.

Strengths

Weaknesses

Opportunities

Threats

Career Priorities

People always ask me how I think I can help everyone land their dream job. At first, I was unsure of this too, but after speaking with thousands of students I realized that people have different goals and aspirations for their career. For some students, money is the most important factor when picking a job. Other students don't care as much about the money as they would rather work for a good cause with a company that has a mission statement they believe in. This is the reason why I added the following assessment to my workbook. I want you to think about what your career priorities are. This is going to be crucial because when you are researching companies you will reference back to this assessment to make sure that the companies you put on your target list fulfill your top three career priorities.

CAREER PRIORITIES

Rank each of the following items in order of importance with #1 being the most important to #10 being the least important.

Experience

Compensation

Company Culture

Company Mission

Growth Potential

Industry

Work Life Balance

PTO/Benefits

Location

Personal Development

MasteringCollegeToCareer.Com

Career Vision

We're continuing on our journey to complete your self-assessment and we've incrementally narrowed down what your dream job could be. For this program to work, it's important to have a focused approach. Based on what you determined from completing the activities above and from your personal research, answer the questions below.

CAREER VISION

Start to narrow down your options by choosing your top industries and companies that you would like to work for.

What are your top 3 industries that you may want to work in? Keep your previous responses in mind and do some additional research on your own in order to best answer this question.

1.

2.

3.

Choose 10 companies that will make up your *Target List*. These should be companies that you would like to work for based on your responses above and your research. The companies on your target list can (and probably will) change over time so don't stress too much about your choices.

1.   6.

2.   7.

3.   8.

4.   9.

5.   10.

This chapter of the book should have given you a lot to think about, but it also should have provided you with clarity. Every activity you completed in this chapter was intentionally designed to help you create an idea of what your ideal life would look like and you should now have a clearer idea of what it will take to get there by narrowing down your top industries and companies. It's important that you are not moving on to the next chapter until you have identified your target list. Don't worry if you are not 100% certain of the companies that you placed on your list. Your list can and will change as you continue throughout your college-to-career journey. It is perfectly normal if you had trouble filling this out. Most students struggle with this part of the program, but you will continue to find clarity along the way. Just make sure that you do your best and write down the top ten companies you want to focus on for the remaining sections.

MY GIFT TO YOU!

Free Access To The Self Discovery Lesson Of My Online Program

This chapter on self discovery sets the foundation for the rest of this program. It's an extremely important chapter which is why I have included a lesson on this topic in the mini course.Here is a link to access the mini course included with the purchase of this book.

Enjoy,

Daniel

Or visit http://bit.ly/mc2cminicourse

CHAPTER 6
FINDING YOUR DREAM JOB IS AN OPEN BOOK TEST

Why Finding Your Dream Job Is An Open Book Test

When I tell students that finding their dream job is an open book test they usually look at me with a strange expression. They don't understand how this can be possible at first, but it is! I'll tell you how by explaining it from the company's perspective.

Imagine that you have graduated and that you are now responsible for hiring all college students for your organization. You have worked with the chief human resource officer and have identified what the entry level position will look like. You have identified the duties and responsibilities for this role, and you have also identified the required hard and soft skills of the job. You have looked at individuals who have held this role or similar roles in the past and you've determined common qualities among the most successful. You then create a job description detailing all of this information. Why would a company go through the trouble to do all of this to not share what they are looking for in their ideal candidate? Don't you think it's in the company's best interest to share this information with every student who is interested in the role? Wouldn't it make sense for the company to tell these students the skills that would make them successful in the role? YES 100%!

Let's also think about why this not only makes logical sense, but it also makes financial sense. I mentioned earlier in the book that I worked for PepsiCo-Frito Lay for six years. On one of my trips to Dallas, Texas to visit the Frito Lay headquarters I had the opportunity to meet with a high-level human resource director. As we were talking, I mentioned that I had been involved with the college hiring program and I was still very passionate about it. As the conversation progressed I asked him if PepsiCo had ever calculated the cost of hiring the wrong person for their sales associate college program role. He told me that it cost PepsiCo $150,000 to hire someone who doesn't stay for at least two years. I was shocked by the answer and I asked him to explain how that could be. He went on to share that you can't just calculate the employee's salary which is an obvious cost, but you also have to add the cost of their benefits, training and development programs, their trainer's salary, their boss's salary and anyone else's salary who spent time working with this employee. This doesn't even include the opportunity-cost of having someone else already trained to do that role. After he explained it this way it all made sense. I was just shocked at how much is at stake when hiring the wrong person. According to a study by the Society for Human Resources Management (SHRM), it could cost up to five times a bad hire's annual salary. In the PepsiCo example, this dollar amount lies between two to three times their first-year salary.

In most cases, companies are investing more money in you as a new hire than what you paid for your college degree. Obviously, that number varies with companies and roles, but the cost is still a lot more than just your compensation. For the majority of companies, employees are their biggest controllable cost. It makes sense why companies have so many steps in the hiring process. They are trying to lower the risk of hiring the wrong person.

Why Finding The Answers To Your Open Book Test Is So Important To You

One of the biggest piece's of advice I give college students is that they can do ANYTHING, but they can't do EVERYTHING. This is a common mistake, especially for students who are overachievers. Frequently, students lack the focus required to become the ideal candidate for their desired companies. As I have shared with you earlier, focus always wins. That is why I had you take the time to complete your self-assessment in the beginning. Don't get me wrong, I do want you to experiment and try new things until you find the one thing that makes you happy and fulfilled, but I also want you to be purposeful and strategic with your actions. As you are experimenting and trying new things, I want you to be all in. As you figure out what is not for you, I want you to move on and continue to narrow down your search until you figure out what your dream job is. There are millions of jobs out there and it's not possible that they're all your dream job. At the same time, it is not possible for you to be the ideal candidate for every job out their either. Why do most students go online and apply for every job possible then? They spend hours and hours applying for hundreds of jobs, hoping to get a call. The reason why they are not getting a call is that the companies reviewing those applications are afraid to hire someone who does not meet their basic requirements. As we learned, new hires are expensive! For a small sized business, hiring the wrong person can even lead to bankruptcy.

Shotgun Vs Sniper Approach

Most students follow the shotgun approach to job searching. They create a generic resume, attend the career fair, and talk to every employer to see if they meet the minimum qualifications. This approach is the same as shooting a shotgun. When you shoot a shotgun you are able to cover a large range, but you are not as accurate. This is why a shotgun is only effective when you are in close proximity to your target, and even then, you don't have much control of your aim. Your career is a long-range shot, which is why you need to use a sniper's approach when it comes to your job search. This approach works just like a sniper's gun would. It is used to hit a target. You have to know where you are aiming and you need to focus on your target. This is the approach that I have all of the students whom I work with use. Now that you have created your target list, you should focus your efforts on becoming their ideal candidate. You can say goodbye to that generic resume because you will create custom resumes for your target companies showing that you are the potential employee they're looking for. This approach will dramatically increase your chances of hitting your ideal target and ultimately land you not just any job, but your dream job.

According to Forbes, 91% of college seniors thought they had the skills to get the job they wanted, but 98% of recruiters said they get resumes from applicants who are not qualified for the position. As you can see, there's a huge disconnect between what college students are doing to prepare for graduation and what companies are actually looking for, but there really shouldn't be! I promise that if you use the sniper approach I just shared with you, you will definitely be qualified for the job. It's important to put yourself in the best position to learn the skills that you need to land your dream job.

Conclusion To Assess

As you can see, there is a purpose for everything that we have covered thus far. My goal has been to help you understand that this is essentially a funnel. As you conduct your self-assessment, gain experience throughout your college career, and learn what you like and dislike, you will have more clarity about your goals and you will ultimately land your dream job. We talked about the importance of taking the time to conduct a self-assessment. It's best to picture what your ideal life looks like and then work backward to figure out how you're going to get there. You completed the activities to gain clarity and give you direction to create your target list of companies. I explained how finding your dream job is an open book test. It is in the company's best interest to tell you what they look for in their ideal candidates. Lastly, I went over the Shotgun vs Sniper approach. In the next chapter we talk about the second step of the program, Acquire. Now that you've already created your target list, I will explain how you should go about getting the answers to your open book test so that you can ensure that you are an ideal candidate.

ACQUIRE

PLAN

CHAPTER 7
HOW TO ACQUIRE THE ANSWERS TO YOUR OPEN BOOK TEST

In the last chapter, we spoke about how landing your dream job is like taking an open book test. The answers are out there for you to find, you just need to know where to look. Since there are millions of companies, that means there are millions of tests. The fact that you have narrowed down your target list of companies that you want to work for will help us understand where to look for your specific answers. I'll explain some great ways to do this. I encourage you to do them all. The more prepared you are, the better off you will be.

Finding The Answers To Your Open Book Test

One of the easiest ways to find the answers to your open book test is to do research on the company and the position you're interested in online. Companies post a lot of this information on their website's career sections and you can usually find relevant information in the job descriptions. This is what most people do. You do get some good information, but you should not stop there. I want you to also look at review websites such as Glassdoor.com. On this website you will be able to get information about salary, you can see reviews from current and past employees, and so much more. I really like this website because it gives you more unbiased answers. You must remember that companies are always going to paint the best picture of themselves and the position on their website. So don't just drink the Kool-aid. Do your research! Read the comments from people who no longer work there. Why did they leave? Was it because it was a toxic work environment? Was it because they had to work on weekends? Was there no room for growth? Regardless of their reason to leave, remember that everyone is different. The reason why someone left a company may be a reason why you should work there. Maybe someone wasn't happy because they had to be at work at six o'clock in the morning. If you're a morning person you may love this because you get to start your day early and leave early. Remember Tony's story. He thought he would love working for a company because his friend loved it, but this is not always the case. Just because someone else disliked the job doesn't mean you will too, but it's definitely something to look into. Take the time to do your research. Your career path is not a decision that should be rushed.

The 10-5-1 Method

Most students conduct online research and think that's enough. It's a good start, but I think you need to go straight to the source to get all of the answers. You should speak to the people who actually do the hiring and the people who are in the role that you're interested in. This activity does take some time to fully complete, but it is absolutely worth it. The good news is that you've already completed the most difficult part by creating your target list. This activity will give you all the answers to your open book test, and it will dramatically increase your chances of landing your dream job. Now let me explain the activity.

I call this activity the 10-5-1 Method. You are going to use the ten companies on your target list and find five people, using

LinkedIn, who work for that company who either hold the position that you're looking to get or hire for that position. It's best to find people who meet these qualifications and also have the most in common with you. For example, you can find someone who attended the same university, likes the same sports team, or is from the same hometown. This is important because you will get a much higher response rate if you find a connection that you can mention. The more unique the connection the better off you will be. When you first find these people, I don't want you to message them right away. Instead, I want you to follow them and spend some time learning more about them. What do they post about? If they don't post, what posts are they engaging with? After you've done that, I want you to start engaging with them by liking and commenting on their posts. You will find that most people are not very active on LinkedIn and their posts probably won't have a whole lot of engagement. This will work in your favor because they will be curious about who you are and they will most likely check out your page. The reason for doing all of this is so that when you send them a personal message they will take the time to read it and reply. The goal is to make sure that you have at least one conversation per company. So ten companies on your target list, connect with five people per company, and have at least one conversation per company. I don't want you to go straight for the kill when you first message these people. It's important to build rapport before you really get into why you're messaging them in the first place. The goal of the first conversation is all about getting them to talk about themselves, their journey, and their experience. You need to position yourself as a curious college student. It is not about coming across as an overachiever and telling them that your dream job is doing what they are currently doing right from the start. You want to let them know that you're currently in the career research stage and you want to learn more. Ask them questions like, *What got you interested in your job?* and, *What makes you successful in your role?*

The more you can get them to talk about themselves, the better. As you build up the relationship, you can start asking questions like what the ideal candidate looks like and what hard or soft skills are required to be successful in their position. You can even go as far as to ask if they would be willing to give you feedback on your resume for this specific position. This is a great way to give them your resume without them feeling pressured to hand it to their HR team. This is also a great way to find out what you need to focus on to be their ideal candidate. This approach will also help you start building an ally. If you take their advice and they can see the changes that you've made or the skills that you've gained they will naturally feel like they have contributed to your success and they will be much more invested in your future. They will be more likely to give your resume to the right person and provide a reference. This is beneficial to them too since most companies have internal referral programs that will compensate them. Companies know that the best hires come from referrals because their employees already know the answers to the open book test and they're able to better identify who will be successful. The 10-5-1 activity is done to help you find the answers to your open book test and to help you find allies who will lead to referrals.

Let me tell you about a student who completed the 10-5-1 activity and really stands out to me. His name is Luis Guzman.

When I started working with Luis he had a clear idea of what he wanted to do after graduation. Luis is very interested in sustainability and his target list consisted of companies that care about the environment. Below is a picture of Luis's LinkedIn at the time he was doing this activity. As you can see, his banner was strategically aligned with the industry in which his target companies are in. He did an amazing job of showcasing that he is all about sustainability.

Luis Guzman · 1st

Corporate Relations, ALPFA UCF

Orlando, Florida

Message   More...

ALPFA UCF

University of Central Florida

See contact info

See connections (500+)

Finance undergraduate student aspiring to become a Finance Operations intern, but open for any position available in the field. Looking forward to acquiring an internship to grow professionally and personally throughout the program. Bilingual conscientious luxury retail Sales Lead/Key-Holder. Effec...

One of the companies on his target list was OUC (Orlando Utility Commission.) They are one of the nation's largest municipal utility companies and they are big on sustainable energy. While conducting his research he found that they had a sustainability summer internship program and he was able to identify the recruiting team that he needed to build a connection with. In the screenshot below you can see that Mary Ellen Nash, the Talent Acquisition Manager for OUC, shared a post about the internship opportunities that OUC had available. Luis was not only the only *student* who engaged with her post, but he was the only *person*. Like I said earlier in the book, most people are not very active on LinkedIn and they don't get much engagement. This is why you will definitely stand out if you complete this activity. If only one person commented and liked one of your posts and you didn't know them, wouldn't you check to see who they are?

Mary Ellen Nash, SHRM SCP, SPHR • 1st
Manager Talent Acquisition - Finding and retaining the best talent
1w

Student intern opportunities available at Orlando Utilities Commission.
Opportunities in data & analytics, engineering, IT and more.

 Orlando Utilities Commission (OUC - The Reliable One)
5,570 followers   + Follow
2w • Edited

Seeking to gain real-world hands on experience? Applications are now being
accepted for an array of internships with OUC. These include Information
Technology, Engineering, Accounting, Data & Analytics, Instructional Design,
Customer Experience and more! Check out OUC.com/careers #OUCproud
#OUCareers #Internships

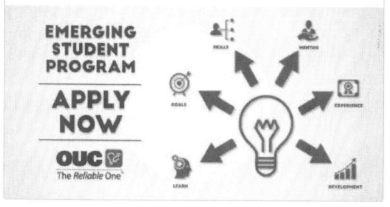

1 Like · 1 Comment

1 Like · 1 Comment

👍 Like   💬 Comment   ➡ Share   Top Comments ▾

Likes

Add a comment...   📷

Luis Guzman • 1st   9h ···
Corporate Relations, ALPFA UCF

Thank you for sharing!

I'm really interested in the Conservation &

Sustainability internship.

I love OUC's goal of powering Orlando \ ...see more

👍 | 💬

A couple of days after this was posted on LinkedIn, OUC had plans to be on Luis's college campus speaking to students about their internship and full-time opportunities. What do you think Luis did? Do you think he attended? Of course, he did. At the end of the presentation, instead of being one of the students asking for more information about the sustainability position he had deeper questions to ask. He even had a personal handwritten card for Emily, the recruiter who oversees the internship program. On top of that, Luis posted a picture on LinkedIn thanking OUC publicly for coming on campus to conduct a workshop and share the opportunities that they had to offer. As you would expect, the talent acquisition team reacted to his post on LinkedIn. He must have made a really good impression!

Luis Guzman • 1st
Corporate Relations, ALPFA UCF
21h

Thank you to Emily Leon, SHRM-CP, CDR, Shantal Irizarry and all the other employers that helped sharpen our professional skills today at the Networking & Interview Workshop.　　　　　　　　　　　　　　　　...see more

31 Likes · 5 Comments

👍 Like　　💬 Comment　　↪ Share

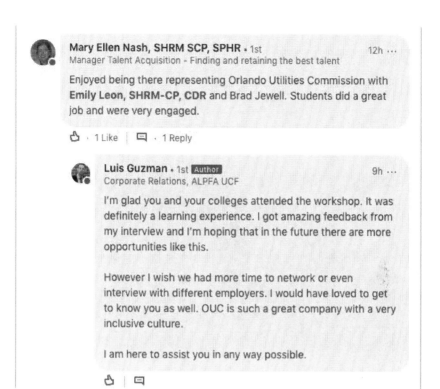

Mary Ellen Nash, SHRM SCP, SPHR • 1st   12h ···
Manager Talent Acquisition - Finding and retaining the best talent

Enjoyed being there representing Orlando Utilities Commission with **Emily Leon, SHRM-CP, CDR** and Brad Jewell. Students did a great job and were very engaged.

👍 · 1 Like   🗨 · 1 Reply

> **Luis Guzman** • 1st Author   9h ···
> Corporate Relations, ALPFA UCF
>
> I'm glad you and your colleges attended the workshop. It was definitely a learning experience. I got amazing feedback from my interview and I'm hoping that in the future there are more opportunities like this.
>
> However I wish we had more time to network or even interview with different employers. I would have loved to get to know you as well. OUC is such a great company with a very inclusive culture.
>
> I am here to assist you in any way possible.
>
> 👍   🗨

All that extra effort Luis put forth did not go unnoticed. For the sake of this example, let me tell you how this story ends. Luis posted a video on LinkedIn talking about my "rules of networking." Haha yes, Luis is so good that he even knows how to build a relationship with me. In this video, you see that he gets a lot of interaction. But more importantly, look at who engages with him. Both Mary and Emily like his video and Emily goes on to write him a comment that tells him, "great video, keep up the good work!"

ALPFA UCF
240 followers
3d • Edited

These 'Rules of Networking' that Daniel Botero shared on his podcast will help you build a genuine and solid connection with anyone you meet.

...see more

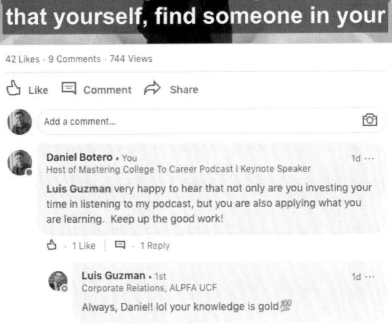

42 Likes · 9 Comments · 744 Views

👍 Like   💬 Comment   ↪ Share

Add a comment...

Daniel Botero • You   1d ···
Host of Mastering College To Career Podcast I Keynote Speaker

Luis Guzman very happy to hear that not only are you investing your time in listening to my podcast, but you are also applying what you are learning. Keep up the good work!

👍 · 1 Like | 💬 · 1 Reply

Luis Guzman • 1st   1d ···
Corporate Relations, ALPFA UCF

Always, Daniel! lol your knowledge is gold 💯

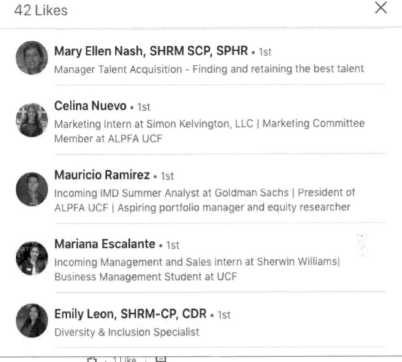

42 Likes ✕

Mary Ellen Nash, SHRM SCP, SPHR • 1st
Manager Talent Acquisition - Finding and retaining the best talent

Celina Nuevo • 1st
Marketing Intern at Simon Kelvington, LLC | Marketing Committee Member at ALPFA UCF

Mauricio Ramirez • 1st
Incoming IMD Summer Analyst at Goldman Sachs | President of ALPFA UCF | Aspiring portfolio manager and equity researcher

Mariana Escalante • 1st
Incoming Management and Sales intern at Sherwin Williams| Business Management Student at UCF

Emily Leon, SHRM-CP, CDR • 1st
Diversity & Inclusion Specialist

♻ · 1 Like 🖂

Emily Leon, SHRM-CP, CDR • 1st   3d ···
Diversity & Inclusion Specialist

Luis Guzman great video, keep up the good work!

👍 · 2 Likes | 🖂 · 1 Reply

Luis Guzman • 1st   3d ···
Corporate Relations, ALPFA UCF

Thank you Emily! 😊 I very much appreciate the kind words

👍 · 1 Like | 🖂

Think about the power of this activity and the doors it can open. Luis started by doing the research and engaging with the right individuals at OUC. These recruiters learned who he was and they even engaged with Luis on his LinkedIn. The story does not end there. Emily was so impressed by Luis that when the job posting went public, she took time out of her busy schedule to personally email Luis the link for him to apply. Not only did Luis get an invite to apply, but he was one of five people to interview for the sustainability internship position. That is the power of the 10-5-1 activity.

Prioritizing Your Target List

Identifying the answers to your open book test starts with knowing which test you are going to take. Once you know which test you're taking (aka what companies you're going to focus on) you can start doing your research and completing the 10-5-1 activity to get your answers. Once you have your answers and know what it takes to be the ideal candidate for your target companies, it is now time to prioritize your target list. Before you actually prioritize your list, I want you to review your responses to the self-assessment questions you completed in chapter five. I want you to make sure the companies on your target list still go hand in hand with your long term goals after you've obtained the information from your research. You also need to make sure that you will be utilizing your strengths in these positions. You need to make sure that you focus on the opportunities that will help you reach your long-term goals and that they also play into your strengths. Once you've done that, it's time to prioritize your list using the ABCD method. I want you to select three companies to be your "A" companies, three companies to be your "B" companies, and three companies to be your "C" companies. You will be left with one company remaining (your "D" company) and you can delete it. Throughout the remainder of the book, I want you to focus on prioritizing your time so you can work on building the answers to your open book test for your A companies. Most of the time your top three companies will be in the same or similar industries and the positions that you are looking at tend to also be very similar.

When you've identified the three "A" companies you intend to focus on, it's time to establish what the most important answers to your open book tests will be. If you get the answers to these questions you should know exactly what you need to do to become the ideal candidate for these top three roles.

To illustrate this example let me show you Jesse Crumbley's LinkedIn. Jesse is a student whom I mentored during his last two years of college. He was an impressive and focused student and it's no wonder that he was able to land such a great job with SAP. He was accepted into their Academy Account Executive program which is more difficult to get into than Harvard.

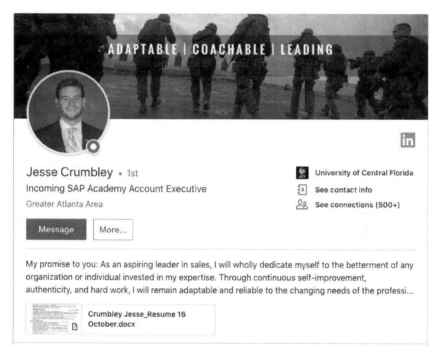

Jesse's dream job was to work in business-to-business sales for a top technology company. After doing his research, he identified the top three qualities that he possesses which would make him the ideal candidate for these companies. He worked strategically to build the skills he needed to stand out. He was also very smart to include a picture of a group of marines in his LinkedIn header which illustrates that he spent time serving in the military.

Jesse did an amazing job promoting himself as the ideal candidate for his target companies. In the next chapter, we will create a plan to take you from where you are now in your journey to the next level. By that point, you should have a clearer idea of what you want to do after college and you should have more answers to your open book test. We will talk about creating a roadmap to help you develop a plan to build the necessary skills to land your dream job.

MY GIFT TO YOU!

Free Access to 10-5-1 The Method Lesson Of My Online Program

In this chapter, you learned about the 10-5-1 Method. This method is the best way for you to find the answers to your open book test. Review this lesson in the mini course to learn more about this topic!

Enjoy,

Daniel

Or visit http://bit.ly/mc2cminicourse

CHAPTER 8
BEING STRATEGIC WITH YOUR TIME

T he most valuable resource in the world is time. It doesn't matter if you're Bill Gates or if you're the guy who picks up the trash, you both start out each day with twenty-four hours. It is how you use that time that makes all of the difference. With that being said, I want to challenge you to use your time wisely while you are in college. The more focused you are in spending your time doing things that will help you reach your goals, the better your chances are that you will walk across the graduation stage with a job lined up. My goal for you is to be strategic with your time. What I mean is that I want you to be intentional. Everything that you do should help you "Acquire" the skills you need to be the ideal candidate. The major that you choose, the student organizations that you join, the community service organizations that you participate in, the internships that you apply for, the professors that you select should all contribute to building the hard and soft skills you will need to impress the recruiters and to help you be successful once you get the job. Let's go into more detail about some of the most important things that you need to be strategic about.

Picking Your Major And Minor

This is a big decision. Within 3 years of initial enrollment, about 30% of undergraduates in associate's and bachelor's degree programs who had declared a major had changed their major at least once. There is nothing wrong with that, but the earlier you can figure out the right major the better off you'll be. One thing that you need to decide is if you want to be a specialist or a generalist. There are some majors that help you build general skills and others that help you build specialized skills. If you plan to be an engineer, for example, then picking your major is not much of a decision. If your goal is to work in business then there are many more options to choose from. You could pick a specialist route like accounting or a generalist route like general business. Both types of majors have their advantages and disadvantages. In most cases, being a specialist will help you obtain a job with a large organization where they are hiring based on their need for those specialized skills. On the other hand, being a generalist will likely help you land jobs with medium and small-sized companies where you may wear multiple hats. There is no right or wrong major. It really is what is the best option for you.

One question I receive a lot from students is whether they should double major or pick up a minor. I think it depends on your goals. If doing this is going to help you be more successful after graduation then I say go for it. Like I mentioned earlier, I double majored. Looking back at my decision, I don't think I needed to do this. I could have saved a lot of money and time if I had only picked one major. From an employer's point of view, a double major or a minor looks good, but it's not something that is required. I don't think it gives you a good return on your investment. It's essentially an extra two words on your diploma. In my opinion, it's more beneficial to be active in student organizations and to hold leadership positions. Many students think that picking up a minor or a double major will help them stand out. This is true to a certain extent, but there are so many other things that you could do to get the same level of benefit without spending so much money and time on extra classes. Again, this is just my personal opinion and everyone's situation is different. I encourage you to do the research to figure out what is right for you.

Being Strategic With Electives And Professors

Not many students put much thought into the electives or the professors that they choose. I want you to take every decision that has to do with your time seriously. Think about this as a game of chess. What move will get you closer to your goal? Electives and professors can help you get there. Most students pick classes based on what is convenient for their schedule. When I say that you should be strategic in the professor that you choose, I don't mean that you should choose the easiest one based off of what ratemyprofessors.com says. I'm saying that you should do research on the professor's backgrounds. I want you to choose professors who have experience in the industries or with the companies that you're interested in. Professors are often well connected in their field. Many become professors after having successful careers. A lot of them also stay connected with past students who could be in a position of power to hire you. I honestly think that building relationships with your professors and choosing classes based on what professors will best help you reach your goals is one of the most underrated things that college students can do. Later in this book, I will go into more detail as to how you can get your professors to become your allies.

Internships

One of the best ways to build the skills needed to land your dream job is through internships. You probably know this by now, but I challenge you to be strategic when choosing internships. To me, there are three main types of internships: discovery internships, experience internships, and foot-in-the-door internships. When I work with students I challenge them to figure out the goal of their internship. What do you want to gain from the experience? Are you choosing an internship to discover if you want to go into that industry? Are you choosing an internship because you are looking to gain more experience and build your skills to help you become the ideal candidate? Are you looking to do an internship with that particular company because that is the company you want to work for after graduation? You could choose an internship for all three reasons, but you should have a primary reason for choosing it.

When I was in college I completed four internships. At the time I didn't know how each internship really fit into those categories, but it helped me receive multiple job offers in the end.

I'll tell you about my internship experience to illustrate my point.

I completed my first internship when I was in my second year in college with Protostar International. I did it primarily to gain experience. I just wanted to get an internship under my belt in order to get future internships that required more experience later on. This qualified as an "experience internship."

My second internship was with Revenue Performance. I was a marketing student at the time and I wanted to explore the digital marketing industry. I have always been fascinated with digital marketing and I thought doing an internship would help me figure out if this was the right industry for me. I feel bad for them because I think I was probably the worst intern that they had ever hired. This wasn't because I was lazy or because I had a bad attitude. I'm not a good writer and the entire internship was about writing blogs. If I'm being completely honest, this book that you are reading right now was probably a nightmare for someone to fix. Spelling and grammar are my biggest weaknesses. This is how I quickly figured out that this industry was not for me. In the end, this internship served as a very good "discovery internship."

My third internship was with Tutor Matching Service (TMS.) This internship allowed me to explore working for a startup company. My goal was to help grow TMS at the University of

Central Florida. This internship served as another great "discovery internship."

My fourth and last internship was with Enterprise Rent-A-Car as a manager-in-training intern. I took this internship because Enterprise was one of the main companies that I wanted to work for. I knew that getting an internship with them would be a great way to get my foot in the door. My plan worked and I was offered a full-time position, but I ended up declining because I received other job offers that were more aligned with my long-term goals. This internship started as a "foot-in-the-door" internship, but it ended up becoming a combination of all three types of internships. I was able to gain a lot of great experience, but I also was able to discover that this company and industry were not as closely aligned with my long term goals as I had once thought.

I challenge you to be strategic with your time and how you pick your internships. Where are you at in your college journey and what do you want to get out of your internship this semester? Do you want to gain more experience and help build those skills your dream companies are looking for? Are you looking for an internship that will allow you to explore and see if this is the industry that you can see yourself building a career in? Are you going to try to get an internship with one of your target companies to get your foot in the door and receive a full-time offer when the internship ends? There is no right or wrong answer. It all depends on where you're at in your college career. The most important thing that you need to do is to make sure you have a purpose.

Job

If you are one of the students who needs to work during college then I challenge you to be strategic about your job. Where you work and what you do with your time are extremely important. I understand completing internships doesn't seem like an option for some people. They have a lot of bills and they're trying to finish school while keeping a full-time job. A lot of people think that they need to complete free internships before you're able to land any good paying internships, but that's not necessarily true. It is a little more difficult to land paid internships if you don't have any experience, but your current job can be the experience that you need. You just need to be able to position it well.

If an internship isn't an option for you, my advice is to find a way to get the experience that you need from your current or future job.

Let's look at an example of a server which happens to be the most common job that college students have. It pays well and they have flexible hours. Let's say that your dream job is to work in one of the management training programs that most Fortune 500 companies offer. The top three qualities that those companies are looking for in these programs are high emotional intelligence, leadership skills, and analytical skills. Since you can't leave your serving job, I want you to think about how you can build those skills while working at the restaurant. Be strategic with your time there. Thinking outside of the box is key. For this example, I would work on building the highest level of customer satisfaction score compared to anybody else at the restaurant. I would make sure that I got customers to write positive reviews on Yelp. I would then take screenshots of those reviews and add them to my career portfolio. I'll speak about career portfolios more later on in the book. Doing this will show that I have great emotional intelligence. These positive reviews showcase my ability to adjust my serving style to each table which is a great indicator of high emotional intelligence. To show leadership skills, I would work with management to become a lead server and see what other leadership roles I could take part in while working there. Remember, you don't need to have the title to lead. You can start with leading by example and being a voice that people listen to. To prove my analytical skills, I would ask my manager to go over the restaurant's analytics with me. Most restaurants have smart point-of-sale systems that track all aspects of the business. I would look at analytics such as the average tip percentage and the percentage of customers who buy desserts or alcohol. I would then see how I could improve these numbers. This will show that I know how to read data, analyze it, and implement solutions.

This is an example of how you can turn a common serving job into a role that gives you the experience you need to become the ideal candidate. If you work in a job that you can't possibly build the skills you need to land your dream job, I would highly encourage you to look for a job that meets your desired income and more closely aligns with your dream job.

Student Organizations

One of the best ways that you can gain experience outside of class and work is by being involved on campus with student organizations. Most universities have hundreds of student organizations. The types of organizations are endless, but I'll talk about some of the most common ones.

Greek organizations, like fraternities and sororities, are popular. There are four main types of greek organizations: social, service, professional, and honor societies. The social fraternities and sororities are what most people think of when it comes to greek life. They are known for their big houses and parties. The service organizations distinguish themselves by making community service and philanthropy their number one focus. The professional organizations focus on professional development and are specific to your major. I was a member of Delta Sigma Pi which is a professional fraternity for business majors. Lastly, honor societies focus on honoring students with high academic achievements. Joining one or several of these organizations is a great way to build the skills needed to become an ideal candidate.

Another type of organization that is great to get involved with are interest-based organizations. These are organizations started based on a common interest. Some examples of these include Advocates for World Health, Art History Club, Chess Club, and the list goes on. Do some research and see what kinds of interest-based organizations there are. You're sure to find at least one that you enjoy. These interest-based organizations are another great way to get involved on campus.

The last type of organization that I'm going to talk about in this book are professional organizations. These are organizations that serve your profession. A couple examples of these include SHRM (Society of Human Resource Managers), ALPFA (Association of Latino Professionals For America), ASCE (American Society of Civil Engineers) for civil engineers. There are hundreds of professional organizations. If you already know what you want to do after college, I highly encourage you to join the organization that serves your future profession or industry. This gives you exposure to individuals who are already doing your dream job. You will have a bigger network that could help you find those answers to your open book test. You will also be able to attend really useful national or regional events where you can network and gain more knowledge about that profession. These events can cost thousands of dollars, but as a student, they are a fraction of the cost if not free. You may be wondering what you should do if your school doesn't have the chapter that you're looking to join. I think this would be a great opportunity for you to be the one to start it. Most of these organizations have processes and resources to help you start professional organizations at your school. It is in their best interest to help you open a chapter as it would help the organization grow.

This creates a win-win situation.

There are many other types of student organizations and I could write a whole book on this topic alone. Though, my goal is not to tell you about each organization that you could join, but I do want you to understand how you can use these organizations in your journey to landing your dream job. The idea is to be strategic with your time by joining organizations that will help you build the skills that you need to be the ideal candidate.

Other

If all of the resources available to students by your school is not enough, you can also find ways to build your skills with what you do outside of school. Think about the sports or hobbies that could help you build the skills that your ideal companies are looking for. Sports are a great way to network and to build leadership and teamwork skills. You can also gain some of those skills with your church or other spiritual organizations. And let's not forget about the internet! You can learn pretty much anything your heart desires by watching YouTube videos or searching the internet. The possibilities are endless.

Learn To Say No And Don't Overextend Yourself

I truly believe that 50% of college is what you learn in the classroom, and 50% is what you learn outside of the classroom. I have spent the last couple of pages of this section giving you ideas on how you can build the skills that you need to land your dream job. Remember, the goal of this chapter is to help you be strategic with your time. It's crucial to use your time, the most valuable resource in the world, doing the things that will give you the best return on your investment. I am not saying that 100% of your time needs to be invested in these activities, but I would recommend that you spend at least 80% of your disposable time on activities that are helping you build the skills you need to land your dream job. If you take the time to do research on what things will be best for you, I think you will find that you will have a lot of fun building these skills. After all, these are skills that will make you successful in your career after college and it's something that you identified as a major interest in your life. You will also find yourself meeting a lot of like-minded individuals who will become lifelong friends. My challenge to you is to learn to say "no" to things that are not helping you reach your end goal. You don't want to overextend yourself. Focus wins. I would much rather you do three things right, be a leader, and be very involved, than doing ten things and not being able to get the most out of your time.

CHAPTER 9
NETWORKING IS KING

Why Networking Is King

It is said that over 85% of jobs are filled through networking. This means that most jobs are filled because someone in the company knew someone who would be a great fit for the job. I don't know about you, but if someone told me that most jobs are filled through networking my next move would be to figure out how to be one of those referrals. The way to do this is through networking. This is why networking is king. The bigger your network, the higher your chances of being referred for positions that you apply for.

Let me share with you the story of Tayler, an individual whom I worked with. Tayler was not happy in his first job out of college. I remember meeting with him for lunch and talking about where he currently stood in his career and where he wanted to be in the near future. After some time he shared that his dream job was to work for Salesforce. I am not sure if you know anything about Salesforce, but they have made the Fortune 100 Best Companies to Work For list for eleven years running and they're currently ranked as the #2 company. As you can imagine this is a very competitive company to get a job with. When Tayler shared with me that this was his dream job, I knew that the only way he would have a chance was by referral. I personally did not know anybody at Salesforce, but I did know someone who was well connected in the tech industry. Long story short, my contact was able to connect Tayler with someone who worked at Salesforce. This eventually helped Tayler land the job. Since getting the job Tayler has shared with me that Salesforce relies heavily on employee referrals to fill their hiring needs.

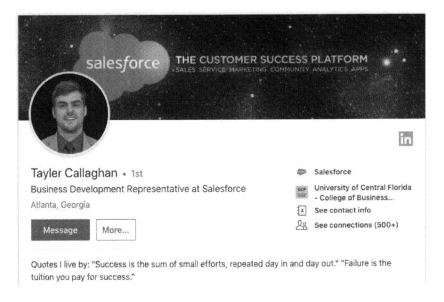

How To Build A Strong Network

I don't get a lot of push back from students when it comes to the importance of networking. What I do get a lot of questions about is how they can build a strong network. I am going to share with you my networking philosophy and how I was able to build a strong network even before I graduated from college. A lot of what I will be sharing with you may sound like common sense, but I promise you that it's not common practice.

Networking is arguably one of the best things that you can do to help you reach your goals. Who you know will help you get your foot in the door, but what you know will keep you there. You can be an expert at something, but without a good network, your opportunities are limited.

Networking definitely doesn't come naturally to everyone so I'm going to share with you my five rules for networking success.

1. Always start with what's in it for them

2. Only receive something when you really need it

3. Make sure you stay top of mind

4. Position yourself as a trusted advisor

5. Don't take more than you need

When it comes to networking, especially with people who are more successful than you, it's all about what's in it for them. You need to be able to provide value for someone otherwise they probably won't stick around for very long. In the beginning, you should try to learn everything you can about them and their goals. While they talk, actively think of ways to help them reach their goals.

After you connect with an individual and provide value, they will most likely want to do something for you in return. This is normal human behavior. Knowing this and learning to accept nothing in return is very important. What you will find is that the more successful the individual is, the more they are asked by others for favors. The fact that you took nothing in return will set you apart and it will dramatically increase your value in their eyes. When the time comes and you need something, they will listen.

Now that you've provided value, it's important that you stay top of mind. You need to make sure that you stay connected, even if it's not always possible to meet with them in person. You can stay connected through phone, email, social media, or handwritten letters for example. Ideally, you want to position yourself as a trusted advisor so that they have more of a reason to stay connected with you, which brings me to my next point.

You may be wondering how you can become a trusted advisor, especially to someone who is more successful than you. I promise that it's possible. Most people don't excel in all aspects of life, so start thinking about what you're really good at. When you meet someone, you should think about what topic you could possibly advise them on in which they might not be as knowledgeable as you. Finding these opportunities and providing this kind of value is key. Be creative, and don't sell yourself short in the areas of life that you are more knowledgeable. Some topics that I have used to position myself as a trusted advisor include millennials, public speaking, personal finance, LinkedIn, and soccer. I may not be an expert in those fields, but I definitely know more about these topics than most people I meet. The key here is to have a good understanding of the other person. You will only get to this point by asking good questions and listening to them.

At the end of the day, we are generally selfish creatures. If someone comes along that does not act selfishly and instead is interested in providing more value than they receive, you will probably want to keep them around. This is why it's crucial that you don't take more than you need. Instead, make sure you go out of your way to provide more value than you receive. Staying on the positive side of the value equation feels good and it gives you confidence that when you do need something, your network will be there to help.

These five rules helped me to build a strong network, and I know that if you apply them you will get the same results.

How To Network At An Event

Now that you know my five rules for networking, I am going to go over how you should network when you are attending an event (or more specifically a networking event.) This will help you make a great first impression with individuals who could help you land your dream job.

I think about networking at an event like I think about playing sports. I break it down into three areas. I have the pregame, during the game, and the post game.

In the pregame, I want to identify what the objective of the event is. What are you trying to achieve at this event? Are you trying to meet a particular person or group of people? Do you want to learn more about the organization that is throwing the event? Or, do you just want to meet new people who have similar interests? You definitely want to do your homework before you attend the event. If the list of attendees is public I would look to see who is attending the event. I would do research using LinkedIn to determine if there are specific individuals whom I want to make sure I connect with before I leave. Once I have done all of this, it is now time to attend the event.

At the event, you want to be strategic. If it's your first time at this particular event, you should first try to connect with the event organizer. This opens up opportunities for you to gain warm referrals. The event organizers are usually one of the best people to network with. Depending on the event, they are probably the most well connected since they put the event together. It's also in their best interest to make sure that you are enjoying your time so that you will come back in the future. A lot of times they will want to know what brought you to the event and what your goals are. They ask these questions so that they can introduce you to people that they think will be good connections for you. This is usually the best way to become introduced to someone. If this is not an option, I would look around to see who's alone and looking to start a conversation. You can also look for groups of individuals that look welcoming and approachable. If they are at a networking event they should be open to a conversation. If not, then why would they be there? When speaking with people remember the five rules of networking covered in the previous section.

Once the event is over, your job is not over. The postgame is where I see the most students fail. They attend the event, speak with all of these people, have a pocketful of business cards, and then they go home and do nothing with them. The reality is that most people fail to follow up. This is the step that really sets you apart. I want you to create a system to follow up. For me, that is writing a personal email to everyone whom I met within the first twenty-four hours of meeting them. If I can find their mailing address I write them a hand-written card. Following up is key if you want to make sure you convert the conversation from a networking event to a mutually beneficial long lasting relationship.

How To Network Using Linkedin

LinkedIn is a powerful tool for building your network and can help you land your dream job. In a later chapter I will cover how to create a LinkedIn profile that will help you stand out, but for now, let's focus on using LinkedIn to build a strong network. The beautiful thing about LinkedIn is that it allows you to build your network strategically. You can target specific individuals that you want to meet. You should follow the same process that you would at an in-person networking event (pre, during, and post.)

The pre-game in this situation is doing more research about the individuals you are trying to connect with. The goal of doing this research is to find commonality. Did they attend the same university as you? Are you from the same home town? Do you love the same sports teams? Do you enjoy the same hobbies? You get the point.

Finding common-ground with these people will increase your chances of them replying.

After you've done your research it's time to start engaging with these people on LinkedIn. Before sending them a message I want you to engage with them by liking and commenting on their posts. After a couple of weeks of doing this then you will send a message.This message needs to be carefully crafted. You want to make sure it's personalized and talks about things that you have in common. You also want to make the message as short and to the point as possible. This is important because people receive multiple messages a day so you want to make yours stand out. I don't know about you, but when I notice that a message was copied and pasted I don't even bother to read it. Here is an example of a message that I sent to Emily, the global marketing director at L'Oreal. I sent her this message because a student whom I was mentoring was interested in working in the beauty industry.

Hi Emily,

I know we've never met but I am the host of the Mastering College to Career Podcast, the goal of the podcast is to help college students have a job lined up before they graduate. I noticed we are both brothers of Dela Sigma Pi. I am currently the District Director (Theta Sigma) University of Central Florida Chapter and I noticed there's a lot of female talent that are interested in the beauty industry. I was very impressed with your background and your experience in the beauty industry and would love to interview you for the podcast and share your story with the student audience because I feel many of them would resonate with your story.

Hope to hear from your soon,

Brotherly,

Daniel

It's Not What You Know Or Who You Know, But Who Knows You

So far in this chapter, we have talked about why networking is king and we've discussed how to build a network both at in-person events and online using LinkedIn. Remember that 80% of jobs are filled by referrals. In order for you to get these referrals, people must know you. They have to know what skills you have to offer and how you would be a good fit for their organization. You want to make sure that while you are building your network, you are positioning yourself as someone people like and trust. People want to know that they won't be let down if they refer you. Most people will say that, "it's not what you know, it's who you know." I think it should really be, "it's not what you know or who you know, but who knows you." It's all about who knows you and who likes and trusts you.

Next is the post-game. Remember that the post-game is all about follow up. If the person did not reply to your message you should send a second one. I would also try to see if you can find their email or phone number and follow up that way. The reality is that most people are not checking their LinkedIn often, particularly if they are happy at their job. If they are not replying, there is a good chance that they did not see your message, so make sure you follow up in other ways.

CHAPTER 10
RUN YOURSELF LIKE A BUSINESS

There have been many times in this book that I have shared examples or asked you to complete activities that would be used when starting a business. It may be because of my entrepreneurial tendencies, but I personally run my life like a business. The point that I want to make is that it helps to run yourself like a business.

What is Your Competitive Advantage?

When you start a business, one of the first things that you do is write a business plan. A SWOT analysis is done at this time which is something that I had you do earlier in the book. The goal of that analysis is to clearly identify your strengths, weaknesses, opportunities, and threats. It is crucial that you are clear about what makes you unique in order to understand why people should invest in you. This especially applies to you now as you are looking for a job. Generally, we spend our whole childhood, especially middle school and high school, trying to fit in. In order to be successful in college, you have to stand out. When growing up, people tend to want to be just like their friends. You'll notice that high school friend-groups tend to dress similarly; the same style, the same type of shoes, the same type of backpack and so on. I am here to tell you that you need to stand out in order to land your dream job.

Think about it. Why would anyone want to hire you if you are just like the rest of the college students? Why would anyone hire someone who hands them a basic resume that is not tailored to their specific company? They can tell that you've probably handed this resume to hundreds of other companies. Companies would rather hire students who stand out for a good reason. They would prefer to hire students who have clarity in what they want their future to look like.

I want you to look at yourself as a business. Successful businesses have clarity in what they are trying to achieve and they understand what makes them different. In other words, they know what their competitive advantage is. Your competitive advantage should be the traits and qualities that make you successful. What do people most admire about you? Is it that you are caring, a great communicator, a very honest individual, or a good listener? I want to challenge you to come up with your three pillars that you will be able to build your personal brand around. This will be how you let others know what your competitive advantage is.

Building A Personal Brand

Now that you have an understanding of what your competitive advantage is and you've identified your three pillars, it's time to build your million-dollar personal brand. Yes, I said million-dollar-brand! You are a million-dollar-brand and you need to treat yourself like one. I once did a podcast interview with Dr. Carolyn Massiah, a marketing professor at the University of Central Florida. In this interview, we spoke a lot about personal branding. One of my biggest takeaways from that interview is how Dr. Massiah said that we are all million-dollar-brands, and she's right! If you earn an average of $50,000 each year for twenty years that means you will have earned one million dollars, making you a million-dollar-brand.

This should give you more of a reason as to why you should take your personal brand seriously. I am not talking about having a Youtube channel or becoming an influencer, but you could. I am talking about making sure that everything you are posting online, every email that you write, every time you meet or talk to someone, everytime you are in public, that you are acting in congruence with the goal of your personal brand. The reality is that we all have a personal brand whether you are trying to build one or not. People have an opinion about you, and that opinion is your current personal brand. Have you ever heard the phrase that perception is reality? Well, that is true now when you are in school and it will be truer once you graduate.

What I want you to do right now is to find out what the perception that people have about you is. What is the brand that you currently have? I want you to contact five to ten people and ask them for their opinion. When you are doing this exercise make sure that you are not just contacting all of your best friends who will tell you what you want to hear. It's helpful to contact a variety of people. Contact people that you don't talk to on a daily basis. This will give you a better understanding of what people are thinking about you and it will allow you to adjust your behavior if you are not happy with what you hear. When I did this assessment, I was a little shocked by the answers. It allowed me to identify things I was doing that I didn't think were a big deal, but that were giving others a sour taste in their mouth about me.

You Are The Average Of The People You Spend The Most Time With

Similarly, like in a business, human capital or the people you surround yourself with will be important. You've probably heard the quote, "birds of a feather flock together," and this is definitely true. You want to surround yourself with people who have similar goals. You want to surround yourself with individuals who will push you to become the best version of yourself. This will be a crucial part of your success in landing your dream job. Make sure that your friends, the individuals that you are spending the most amount of time with, are the right people who will push you, motivate you, and pick you up if you fall. If you ever feel like you can't share your successes with your friends because they will think that you are showing off then you need to find new friends. This can be very difficult, especially if you've known some of those friends for a long time. I see this become an issue a lot when you're attending the same college as your high school friends. I am not saying that you need to stop talking to them completely, but you should try to minimize your time around them.

Creating A Board Of Directors

Most companies and large organizations have a board of directors that help guide the company's direction. They are responsible for the top level strategies that the CEO is responsible for executing. Most companies have a very diverse board of directors comprised of distinguished individuals who are experts in a particular area that is important to the business. The board members usually meet a couple of times each year when they're not bogged down by the day to day operations of the business. This same model is something that I want you to apply to your life. I want you to create your own board of directors. Your board of directors can be filled with your mentors and advisors of the most important areas of your life. There is no specific number of board members and you don't need to have them all meet in the same place at once. The goal is to choose individuals who are knowledgeable in the different areas of life that are important to you. You don't need to speak to these people daily, but you should be able to give them a call if a question comes up or you need advice. Some of the areas in my life that I have board of directors or mentors for are public speaking, fitness, relationships, spiritual, business, finance, and many more.

Managing Your Personal Finances

This is not a book about personal finance, but since we are in the chapter of running like a business, I want to take a few minutes to talk about this important topic as it relates to college students. The decisions that you make now with your finances will impact you for the rest of your life. Student loans are a topic that I feel should be covered. The fact of the matter is that student loans are the easiest way to borrow money, making it a very slippery slope. I highly suggest staying away from student loans if you can. The average college student is graduating with over $30,000 in student loans. Those monthly payments will definitely be a burden, and it's not worth it. Make sure that you apply for scholarships. There are so many scholarships out there, and most people won't take the time to apply for them. This is easy money. If you still need money, try picking up a part-time job to minimize the loan amounts. Trust me; I get it. I graduated with over $20,000 in student loan debt. My rule of thumb is that you should only take out student loans if you have no other options. If you do end up taking out student loans, use the money to only pay for tuition. Don't make the mistake of taking out loans to pay for living expenses or anything besides tuition. Trust me on this one!

CHAPTER 11
TAKING ADVANTAGE OF THE
STUDENT CARD

In this chapter I want to dive into some of the biggest benefits you have just by being a student. I refer to this as your student card. There are so many benefits to being a student!

Career Services Department

Most schools have a career services department. This department offers different services depending on the size of the school and the number of resources allocated to the department. The main thing that I want you to take away from career services is that they are there to help you land your dream job. It is in their best interest to help you land a job and be successful.

Let's take a look at this department from their point of view. Their goal is to get students placed after graduation. Why is this important? This is important to them for multiple reasons. One of these reasons is that a school's reputation is closely aligned with how well the school is able to prepare its students for life after graduation. Are the students graduating with jobs and are those jobs with great companies? Are the students getting a good return on their investment? If the answer is yes to these questions then those students who have found great jobs become successful alumni. Successful alumni donate money and they speak highly about their school which leads to an increase in admission and more money for the school to continue to grow. Career services wants to make sure that you become one of those successful alumni. This is why I encourage every student to work with their career services department. You can start working with them as early as your freshman year. You would begin with career guidance where they can help you create your first resume and they'll even practice mock interviews with you and much more.

Sometimes people think that I'm trying to act as a replacement for the career services department, but this isn't true at all. In fact, it's actually the opposite. I want students to take advantage of all that this department has to offer. I want you to get all the free help you can get. If you need more help and direction then I am here and happy to help. This book, the services that I provide, and all of my other resources are meant to be complementary to what career services has to offer.

Within career services there is a department called employer relations. This department is responsible for managing the relationships with the companies that hire from their school. They are always reaching out to new companies to recruit at their school. The more companies that recruit, the more jobs that will be available for students.

Now that you know all of this, I encourage you to take advantage of their services. Here is an advanced trick that you can use to land your dream job. Once you have created your target list and your college road map, I want you to set up a meeting with the person responsible for your particular major in the employer relations department. I want you to share your target list with them. They know all of the decision makers for these companies that you're interested in and they will be able to give your resume to the right person. We'll talk more about this in a later chapter. If they don't happen to have a relationship with any of your target list companies they will likely reach out to them on your behalf. They will probably share your resume as an example of the students those companies can find if they recruit at your school. Remember that the employer relations department is always looking for new companies to recruit at their school. Since you have already done your research and your resume illustrates this, the companies should be impressed. This becomes a great win-win situation for both you and the employer relations department.

There are many more resources available within your career services department. Please make sure to check them out and tell them Daniel from Mastering College to Career sent you. This may get them to hire me to come speak at your school.

Professors And Faculty

Professors and Faculty are sometimes overlooked by students. I see this happen much more at large universities where the professors are teaching hundreds of students each semester. To me, this becomes a great opportunity. When a crime occurs in public and many people see it, most people won't call the police because they think someone else will. On the other hand, if a crime occurs and you are the only person to see it, you will make sure to call the police. This is similar to how students view their time with professors. When professors have hundreds of students, most students will think that the professors are busy with questions and that they get a lot of office hour visits. I have spoken with so many professors and they all tell me the same thing. Most students don't take the opportunity to get to know them.

Most colleges and universities mandate that all professors have set office hours in which the professors must make themselves available for students. The reality is that unless it's right after a test, students are not taking advantage of those office hours. Even if you don't have any questions about the classes that you are taking, I encourage you to go and build a relationship with your professors. Go and ask them what they're currently working on. Ask them if they're doing any research that you might be able to help them with. You will be surprised at how many doors can open when you build good relationships with your professors.

This is something that I did very well while I was in college. I was not the best student, but I did make sure to build relationships with my professors. I still talk to many of them today and we have amazing mutually beneficial relationships. Many of them have even been guests on my Mastering College to Career Podcast. My challenge to you is to introduce yourself to your professors on the first day of class. Let them know that you're excited to be in their class. I want you to sit in the front row and ask a lot of questions. Also, don't forget to visit office hours a couple of times each semester.

When you do this, you will see how quickly you will be able to build strong relationships that could lead to you getting a letter of recommendation, a scholarship, an internship, and even your dream job.

Student Government Association

Do you know what SGA (student government association) is and what they do? They are the voice of the students. Student government is generally run like the United States federal government. Elections are held every year for President, Vice President, Senate and many other positions. The goal of student government is to be the voice of the student body to the university. They are also responsible for one of the largest discretionary budgets the university has. This budget is used to enrich students' time while attending the university. On top of the major benefits that you can gain from being involved in student government in terms of experience, there are hundreds of other benefits that most students do not know about. On one of the episodes of the Mastering College To Career Podcast I interviewed Josh Boloña who, at the time, was the SGA president at the University of Central Florida. In this episode, we spoke about some of the great things SGA offers their students. Here are a couple of examples offered at UCF. They provide a state of the art gym and sports fields, transportation from school to nearby student housing, free legal counsel, free photocopiers, discounts to attractions, concerts, and other entrainment. One of my favorite things that they do is help to fund student enrichment activities. This means that if you want to attend a conference like the Mastering College To Career Seminar you can apply to get it funded by SGA. This is beneficial because there are many large conventions and career fairs that are expensive, but students can attend with the help of SGA.

I do want to point out that these services are not free and are, in fact, part of your tuition and fees. Make sure you take advantage of this because a lot of students don't. You're already paying for this whether you like it or not so make sure you get your money's worth!

Getting Meetings With Professionals

Imagine you are playing soccer with your friends and there is a little kid watching you play. After the game is over the little kid walks up to you and asks if you can show him how to kick the ball. What would you tell him? Unless you are the Grinch you most likely will tell him yes and help him for a couple of minutes.

This is the same when you, as a student, reach out to professionals who are currently working in your dream job. Again, unless they are the Grinch they will take a couple of minutes of their time to talk to you about what they do and how they got to where they are. This is truer when you are a student than once you graduate. This is why it's important to reach out when you are still a student. People want to help students. They want to be part of your success story.

This applies even more when you have something in common with these individuals. Take advantage of your school's alumni network. They are a great place to start.

Professional Organizations

Earlier in the book, I spoke a lot about being involved on campus and how many professional organizations have student chapters (i.e. SHRM, SHPE, etc.) Now I want you to take it a step further. I want you to attend the local chapter meeting of the professional organizations that interest you. I am part of a couple local professional organizations and it's rare that I see a students attend the monthly meetings. The few times that I have seen students at these meetings they always receive so much positive attention. Most of the time they are able to join at a discounted rate, if not get the membership for free. Your network will increase dramatically and you will learn what is currently going on in your desired field. This is a great way to get mentors and a great way to land your dream job.

As you can see, there are a lot of benefits to being a college student. There is no better time to build a solid network than when you are in college. Make sure you take full advantage of what your school has to offer!

Conclusion To Acquire

Congratulations, you have reached the end of the Acquire chapter of the book! Implementing what you have learned from this section is what will make or break you. If you have not already done so, make sure you complete your self-assessment. It's important that you have clarity as to what your target list of companies is and that you've created your college roadmap. Don't put it off! Start applying what you've learned in this chapter immediately. Network, run yourself like a business, work on your million-dollar personal brand, and take full advantage of your student card. Use the resources available to you at career services, SGA, and all the other outside resources not found at your school. In the next chapter of the book, we cover the last step of the program; Achieve. We continue to talk about more ways that you can stand out and ultimately reach the end goal of landing your dream job.

ACHIEVE

In this chapter of the book, we will focus on crossing that finish line. This is the last mile of the marathon, but this last mile will be crucial. The goal is to make sure that you're walking across that graduation stage with not just a diploma, but with a job offer from one of your target companies. By the end of this section, you will know how to stand out among the crowd with the right tools. We will go over how you should market yourself online and offline to take your million-dollar-brand to the next level. You will learn how to approach employers and build relationships with the decision makers, turning them into your advocates. We will cover some basic resume techniques that will help your resume stand out both to an applicant tracking system and a recruiter. Lastly, we will talk about the interview and how to follow up after the interview. Let's get started so you can achieve your goal of landing that job!

CHAPTER 12
STANDING OUT AMONG THE CROWD

What Sells Better? A Good Product That Is Poorly Marketed Or A Bad Product That Is Marketed Well?

If you have heard of any of my Mastering College To Career keynotes you know that I ask the crowd the following questions. What sells better? A good product that is poorly marketed or a bad product that is marketed well? I always get a couple of people who tell me that a good product will sell better. I want you to really think about it though. How can that product sell better if no one knows about it? Think about it in another way. How many times have you seen people who are not as talented as you achieve a goal that you want to achieve? How did they get that opportunity over you?

I've seen this a lot over the last couple of years. I have had a goal of building my public speaking career for a long time now. I would attend events and hear public speakers talk. Some of them were fantastic, and others I wondered how they were the ones on stage and I was not. This is what got me thinking. How were there people less talented, less driven, or less knowledgeable doing the things I personally wanted to accomplish? How were they doing all of these things and I was sitting on the sidelines? The reason is that they marketed themselves well which helped them to stand out and get noticed.

This applies to you too. There are students who are less talented and less knowledgeable than you receiving offers from your dream companies because they marketed themselves well and they stood out. You have worked hard to get this far, so make sure you don't stop now. In the rest of this chapter I will talk about how you can stand out among the crowd which will lead to you the opportunities you deserve.

Business Cards

Do you have a business card? As a student, you should create a business card. Having business cards is important because it will allow you to exchange contact information with people you meet at networking events or other unexpected places. If you are looking to get someone's information in a professional setting you will ask them for a business card. Naturally out of courtesy they will ask you for yours so make sure you are prepared. You don't need to have expensive business cards. You can get them done online for less than $20 and they will work just fine. All you need is your name, the school that you attend, your major, your expected graduation date, your phone number, and your email. I would also add a LinkedIn link. Here are a couple of examples.

The first example is of my business card while I was in college.

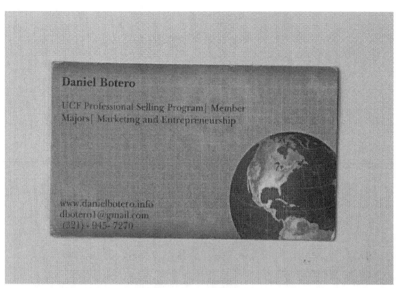

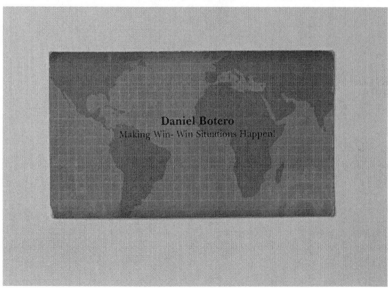

Jessica Rose Lupo

Professional Selling Program Member
Integrated Business | University of Central Florida

www.JessicaLupo.com | 321.848.████ | JessicaRLupo@gmail.com

IF IT DOESN'T CHALLENGE YOU,
IT DOESN'T CHANGE YOU.

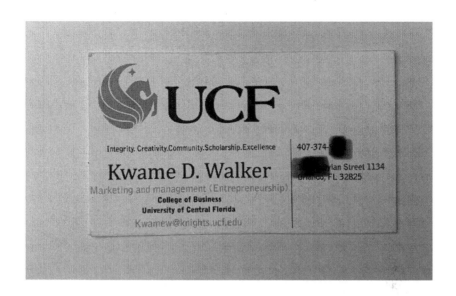

Thank You Cards/Stationary

We live in a digital world. Everyone tries to do everything as efficient and as fast as possible. We live in a world of copy and paste. But what if you did the exact opposite? What if you wrote handwritten thank you cards to everyone you met in a professional setting? Would that set you apart? It absolutely would. Few people, let alone students, write handwritten letters. This is something I learned while in college and it has helped me connect with people that I would not have expected to reply. Writing a letter is also a great way to follow up after an interview. This little investment can open many doors. You can also find stationary online and it's simple to customize. I would keep it simple and professional. Here are some examples of stationary some students that I have worked with have sent me over the past few years. I always keep them, so when you graduate with a job don't forget to send me one!

Daniel,
What can I even say?
Thank you isn't enough....
DSP, PSP, and now the chance to
work on this team and develope your
dream. I am excited and can't wait
to kill it with you this semester!
I look at you as a friend, mentor, and
brother - Thank You! #PTBAD

Chad White   ChadMichaelWhite.com   321-544-

118

Hey Daniel!

I wanted to take the time to show my appreciation to you in assisting me finding a new opportunity. I am truly excited in working with Curtis and helping AMcards.com grow to new heights. Thank you again for all your efforts and helping me discover a new venture within my professional career!

-Abraham Vasconez

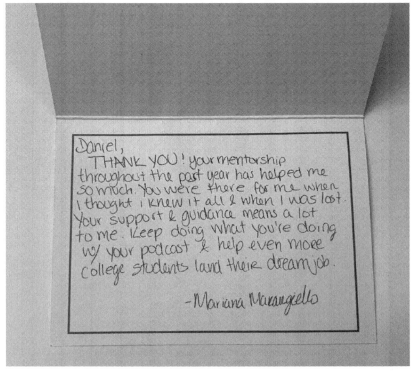

Daniel,

THANK YOU! your mentorship throughout the past year has helped me so much. You were there for me when I thought i knew it all & when I was lost. Your support & guidance means a lot to me. Keep doing what you're doing w/ your podcast & help even more college students land their dream job.

-Mariana Marangiello

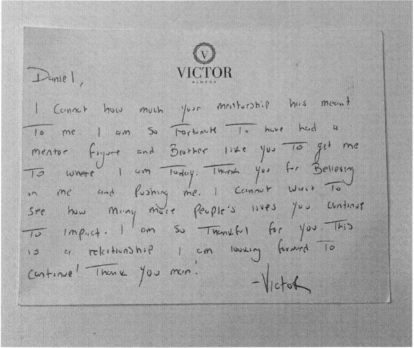

Daniel,

I cannot how much your mentorship has meant To me. I am so fortunate To have had a mentor figure and Brother like you To get me To where I am Today. Thank you for Believing in me and Pushing me. I cannot wait To see how many more people's lives you continue To impact. I am so Thankful for you. This is a relationship I am looking forward To continue! Thank you man!

— Victor

Dear Daniel,

Thank you for being so accessible. I can't thank you enough for guiding me through my career path. I know there's so much for me to get done in order to land my dream job @ Tesla, but I know that if I listen to you; I'll be one step closer.

I promise that I will put in the work & go above & beyond. Thank you for being such an amazing host & friend.

Much Love,

Luis ☺

Lastly, here is an example of Karla Santiago's business card and thank you card combo. Look how good it looks when they both match!

Career Portfolio

Many majors in the arts have their students create a portfolio to showcase their work. This is a great concept and I think every student should create one. You may not have anything to put in it now, but I promise you will. Taking a career portfolio to an interview will allow you to stand out and dramatically increase your chances of landing the job. Imagine sitting in an interview and the recruiter asks you to share an example of when you have gone above and beyond for a customer. Instead of just sharing an example verbally, you flip through your portfolio and show them an actual example of your work. This simple act will impress the recruiter and it will show them that you're not exaggerating your response. Even if they don't ask you anything that prompts you to open your portfolio, the fact that there is this portfolio on the table will drive curiosity and they will ask to see it. Just having it shows them that you are prepared and that you take your job search seriously.

Here are some of the items I suggest you have in your portfolio:

- Resume

- Cover Letter

- University Transcript

- Letters of Recommendation (from your professors, managers, peer leaders in student organizations, etc.)

- Awards or Recognitions (scholarships, dean's list, superlatives, etc.)

- Proof of Community Service

- Examples of Past Work (group projects, research papers, presentations, etc.)

- Books that you've read

- Anything else that makes you stand out

If you would like to see a couple of examples visit MasteringCollegeToCareer.Com/bookresources

Website

We are in a digital age and there is a website for just about everything. Because of that, I want you to create your own website. It does not have to be a complicated website. Your website will act as your digital portfolio. It can have the same components as your career portfolio, but I do want you to remember one thing. When people are looking at your career portfolio they will be with you. This will give you the opportunity to answer any questions that they may have. When someone is looking at your website they won't be with you. This means that you will need to add explanations for each item on your website. I encourage you to include a video sharing more about you and your why. I also want you to make sure that you have plenty of pictures. People who visit your website should be able to figure out who you are as a person, what you have accomplished so far, and what you are trying to do in the future.

Standing Out Online

Have you ever googled yourself?

If not, this is something you need to do. You should also set up google alerts so that you're notified if your name shows up on Google. You need to know what others see when they search for you online. I want you to stand out online for positive reasons only. Not all employers will Google their candidates, but some will. Remember it is a big investment when they hire you.

Let's start by focusing on social media. I want you to focus on developing a social media strategy. You should post content that adds value to your brand. Every post that you create will either add value to your personal brand or it will take away value. There is no such thing as a neutral post so be strategic about that. I also want you to remember that everything you put on the internet will live forever on the internet and it can be found. Please be careful with that. For the purpose of this book, I am only going to go into detail about LinkedIn. LinkedIn is so crucial to your job search that the next chapter is dedicated to this topic. For the rest of this chapter, I will touch on other social media platforms and how to make sure that they do not kill your chances of graduating with a job.

More recruiters and talent acquisition managers are looking at students social media before setting up an interview. They are not just looking at LinkedIn. They are looking at all social media platforms before making a decision to meet with you or not. Many professionals that I meet with say that students should freeze or delete their accounts while looking for a job, but I don't agree with this. I think that shows recruiters that you have something to hide. I think you should show your life, but just be mindful of what you post. Don't post pictures with drugs or you in an intoxicated state. It is okay to post a picture with a beer in your hand at a tailgating event, but keep it PG. Employers still want to see that you have a life, that you are social, and that you have relationships. Remember people hire people they like, trust, and can relate to.

CHAPTER 13
ACHIEVING SUCCESS THROUGH LINKEDIN

LinkedIn is a professional social media platform that continues to grow. It is crucial to make sure you spent a lot of time building your LinkedIn profile as it will become your digital resume. The reality is that your profile will be viewed more than your resume, so make sure that you are strategic in what you choose to include on your profile. This will be the difference between people reaching out to you about jobs or not. Let's focus on some of the things that will help your LinkedIn profile stand out. Let's start from the top of your profile.

Building Your Profile Picture And Banner

The first thing that people see when going on your page is your profile picture. I see many students use a cropped picture of them at an event where they were dressed professionally. I need you to do better than that. If you can afford to do so, get a professional headshot done. You can check with your career services department because most schools will bring in a photographer at least once each semester to take headshots. A professional headshot makes a big difference because people will take you more seriously. They will likely assume that if your picture is professional that you will act professionally too. I also want you to change the banner. Take advantage of that space and add something that tells the people looking at your page more information about you. Let's look at two different examples.

IF IT DOESN'T CHALLENGE YOU, IT DOESN'T CHANGE YOU.

I took a screenshot of the profile pictures and banners of two students. Just by looking at these pictures you can learn a lot about each student. I am sure that the student in the first picture is a nice guy, but the young lady in the second picture definitely looks more professional. Most people would gravitate toward starting a conversation with her than with the student from the first example.

The person in the second picture is a student I mentored named Jessica Lupo. I would highly encourage you to look at her LinkedIn profile as she does a very good job showcasing her self, her experience, and much more. Kudos to Jessica!

Headline And Summary

After your picture and your banner, the next thing that you need to focus on is your headline. This is important since it shows when people search you, along with your picture and your name. Your headline needs to be keyword optimized and it needs to express what you currently do or what you want to do. You want people to find it so intriguing that they want to click on your page to learn more. After the headline comes the summary. The summary is very important, but it's one of the sections that is the most under-utilized. I encourage you to share information about yourself and include things that people who don't know you would want to know. The goal is to have others get to know you better. Unlike the headline that allows just 120 characters, you are allowed 2,000 characters in your summary. Make sure you use these words wisely. Your summary should also be keyword optimized. This section will help you get your ranking higher on keywords that you want to be found on. I could write a book on this subject alone, but I will tell you that William Arruda wrote a great article teaching you step by step how to write a compelling LinkedIn summary. I highly encourage you to read it. Just to help show you what a good LinkedIn summary looks like, I have posted a picture of mine below. P.S. Let's connect on LinkedIn!

Daniel Botero 🔗

College to Career Transition Expert I Top Rated Podcast
Host I Speaker I Author of Mastering College To Career
Book

Orlando, Florida Area · 500+ connections · Contact info

Mastering College To Career

University of Central Florida

About

I found my dream job helping others find their dream job. I pride myself in the fact that I've helped hundreds of individuals land their dream job. In fact, every student that I've worked one on one with, has gotten at least one job offer before graduation.

I have my own podcast called "Mastering College To Career" It has over 75 episodes and it's rated 5 stars on Itunes. Check it out to get great tips on how to land your dream job! I not only provide my own advice, but I also interview industry experts and students. I publish new episodes every Monday and Thursdays!

Networking is my thing. I love building relationships and connecting the dots to create win-win situations. When I meet someone new, I'm always thinking about how I can bring value to the relationship.

I had a successful career with a Fortune 50 company before deciding to work full time on my dream job. I held 4 different roles in 6 years and managed over $100 Million in yearly sales across the Southeastern United States. I never missed a sales plan, in fact I regularly tripled company performance.

I'm committed to being a lifelong learner. I make sure that I'm educating myself and always growing. I've read or listened to over 500 nonfiction books in the past 10 years. Even though I've read hundreds of books and I've learned more than most people have forgotten, there are some areas that I can't seem to get grip on. One of these areas is writing. If you've read this far and you think that this is very well written, it's because my wife helped me write it.

I encourage you to read the recommendations that people have given me. These people include past managers and professors, business professionals, and students that I've helped land their dream job.

Specialties:#LinkedIn #podcasting #CollegeStudents #CollegeHiring, #TalentAcquisition, #KeynoteSpeaking, #Recruiting, #Sales, #Business #Development, #Entrepreneurship

As you will notice from my summary, I talk about what I currently do. I help others students transition from college to career. I talk about having my own podcast. I share that I love networking and I am always thinking of helping others. I go on to share more about my corporate career to help build some credibility. Then I use a technique called "extraordinary and ordinary." I share something

130

extraordinary that I did like reading over 500 books and then I talk about my weakness of not being a good writer. This allows people to get to know me better. I then send people to read my recommendations since I have a lot and it will add more social proof. My goal with my summary is for people who don't know me to feel like we have known each other for years. I want to make sure I sound approachable and like I'm always looking to connect.

Now let's talk about an example of a student I mentor, Luis. You may remember Luis because I talked about him earlier in the book when I explained how he connected with the talent acquisition department of OUC. Let's review his LinkedIn summary.

Luis Guzman · 1st

Finance Intern at Universal Creative | Finance Student

Orlando, Florida · 500+ connections · Contact info

Message | View in Recruiter | More...

Universal Creative

University of Central Florida

Highlights

783 Mutual Connections
You and Luis both know Elizabeth Caraballo, SHRM-CP, Jan Miller, and 781 others

Luis started a new position as Finance Intern at Universal Creative

Say congrats

About

The most interesting thing about me is not that I attend UCF to get a Finance degree, it's how I got here and how I am continuously developing myself.

I am an international student from Mexico City. I left my family behind and came with nothing but a suitcase. I got one shot and I WILL make sure to make all my sacrifices are worth it.

On my first job, I developed leadership skills that allowed me to be creative at finding strategic solutions to solve problems. I also learned to understand different types of personalities to work with diverse individuals. While working in luxury retail, I became dedicated to providing a relationship-oriented experience to build long-lasting relationships.

I am extremely passionate about the environment and volunteering. My dream is to work for a company that is socially and environmentally responsible. I currently volunteer at Orange County Animal Services and #HashtagLunchBag Orlando. At the animal shelter, I apply my sales skills to find the right home for pets by practicing active listening. With #HashtagLunchBag I put together lunches for homeless people and then give them away. This not only keeps my heart warm, but it also makes me appreciate everything I've been blessed with.

I want to start my career in Corporate Finance as a Financial Analyst for three years. Go back to school while still working to get my MBA and move on to Risk. Lastly, I'd like to do Operations to have a full understanding of the field. The goal is to be a CFO one day. It is a long road, but I am willing to put the work into it.

#Finance #Analysis #FinancialAnalyst #Volunteer #Sustainability #Tesla #Solar #Student

 Resume.docx

 About me.docx

Luis starts off his summary talking about how he is more than just a finance student at UCF and he explains his story. He talks about what he learned in his first job, where he currently volunteers, and what he has learned with this experience. Lastly, he goes on to share his goals and aspirations. This shows employers that he knows what he wants his life to look like five to ten years from now and he's taking action to make it happen. He also attached his resume and a document that tells more about himself in this section. Great job Luis!

I think this section is really important so I'm going to give you another example of a student's LinkedIn profile. My hope is that these examples will give you some ideas for your own LinkedIn profile.

This next LinkedIn profile is from another student that I have mentored, Chad White. He has one of the best student LinkedIn profiles that I have seen in a while.

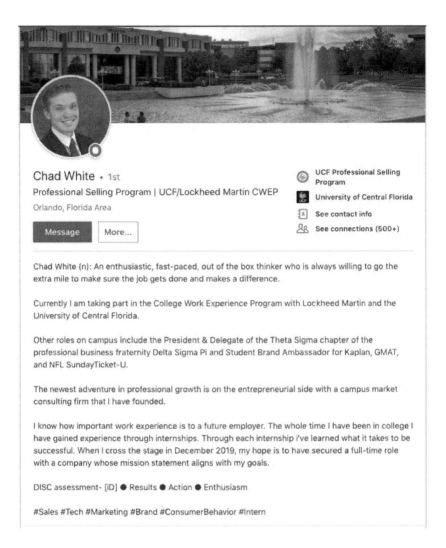

Chad White · 1st

Professional Selling Program | UCF/Lockheed Martin CWEP

Orlando, Florida Area

Message   More...

UCF Professional Selling Program

University of Central Florida

See contact info

See connections (500+)

Chad White (n): An enthusiastic, fast-paced, out of the box thinker who is always willing to go the extra mile to make sure the job gets done and makes a difference.

Currently I am taking part in the College Work Experience Program with Lockheed Martin and the University of Central Florida.

Other roles on campus include the President & Delegate of the Theta Sigma chapter of the professional business fraternity Delta Sigma Pi and Student Brand Ambassador for Kaplan, GMAT, and NFL SundayTicket-U.

The newest adventure in professional growth is on the entrepreneurial side with a campus market consulting firm that I have founded.

I know how important work experience is to a future employer. The whole time I have been in college I have gained experience through internships. Through each internship I've learned what it takes to be successful. When I cross the stage in December 2019, my hope is to have secured a full-time role with a company whose mission statement aligns with my goals.

DISC assessment- [iD] ● Results ● Action ● Enthusiasm

#Sales #Tech #Marketing #Brand #ConsumerBehavior #Intern

As you can see Chad has a professional headshot, he takes advantage of the banner by having a picture of his university, and he has written what he's currently involved in in the headline which will help him rank higher in searches. All of these things are great, but let's focus on his summary.

He starts out by giving a definition of himself. He points out his competitive advantage which is something we talked about earlier in the book. Then he goes on to talk about where he currently works and what other leadership positions he holds on campus. This

134

summary lets people who read this know that he is involved and he has a lot of leadership skills. He goes on to share his goal and leaves a note to future employers. He also shares the results of his DISC assessment. This is great since it lets employers looking at his summary know two things. First, it lets them know that he is self-aware of his strengths and weaknesses. Second, it allows employers to see if they have any jobs that match his assessment. Finally, he finishes off with strategic keywords that will help employers find him due to the LinkedIn algorithm. Well done Chad! Major kudos to you, my friend.

Experience

Next, let's talk about the experience portion of the LinkedIn page. This needs to be similar to your resume and the dates need to match. You may have more information here than on your actual resume since you have more space, but it's important that the dates match. Here are the top takeaways from this section. Make sure you describe the role or positions held and then use bullet points to highlight key achievements. Like your resume, the more you can quantify your success the better you will be in the long run. Let's go over some examples.

Student X

Financial Representative
Northwestern Mutual
Apr 2018 – Sep 2018 · 6 mos
Orlando, Florida Area

Server
Applebee's Neighborhood Grill + Bar
Jul 2016 – Jul 2017 · 1 yr 1 mo
Orlando, Florida Area

Associate Trainer
Panera Bread
May 2014 – May 2016 · 2 yrs 1 mo
Orlando, Florida Area

As you can see from this example, this particular student had good experience. You can tell just by looking at where he worked and the positions that he held. He did not take the time to go into detail on each role though. He didn't explain what his duties were and he didn't tell us any of his accomplishments. Taking the time to include this information would make a world of a difference for him in the long run.

Student: Karla Santiago

Experience

Sales Campus Intern
CDW•G
Mar 2018 – Present · 1 yr 2 mos
University of Central Florida

• Assisted in generating upwards of $100,000 in potential sales for the account from April 2018 to October 2018.
• Created an in-depth video tutorial that is used during the programs on-boarding process of over 30 new interns every year.
• Placed in the Top 10, out of more than 50 interns, in their annual sales scavenger hunt.
• Serve as an effective hands-on liaison between UCF, the CDW Sales team and their various Fortune 500 technology partners.
• Conduct research on relevant technology trends that serve as opportunities for CDW strategic advancement on campus.
• Conduct constant face-to-face networking, building and maintaining relationships with existing and prospective customers across the various departments on campus. See less

Smart Sheet Intern
On-boarding Tutorial

Delta Sigma Pi
1 yr 4 mos

Brother
Mar 2018 – Present · 1 yr 2 mos
University of Central Florida

Delta Sigma Pi is a professional fraternity organized to foster the study of business in universities; to encourage scholarship, social activity and the association of students for their mutual advancement by research and practice; to promote closer affiliation between the commercial world and students of commerce, and to further a higher standard of c...
See more

Chancellor
Apr 2018 – Dec 2018 · 9 mos
University of Central Florida

• Efficiently and effectively coordinated and lead various meetings of more than 70 people.
• Designed shirts that generated over $1000 in profit.
• Worked as part of the executive team to strategize the general vision and monetary goals of the collegiate chapter.... See more

Pledge Class Chancellor
Jan 2018 – Mar 2018 · 3 mos
Epsilon Eta - UCF

• Worked as part of the executive team to strategize the general vision and monetary goals of the pledge class as a whole during its 8-week lifespan.
• Efficiently and effectively coordinated and lead various meetings of more than 20 people.

Here is a great example of an experience section from a student that I mentor, Karla Santiago. She does a great job summarizing the roles that she's had and then using bullet points to list the highlights. This section is called "Experience" and not "Job History" for a reason. Look how Karla showcases her involvement in a student organization. It shows growth and progression. Being part of a student organization gives you experience and you should treat it as a job! The more information, the better. Give people looking at your profile the choice to read more if they want. Kudos to Karla for a great Experience section on her LinkedIn profile!

Education And Licenses & Certifications

The next section on the LinkedIn profile is Education and Licenses & Certifications. This section allows you to show off all of the training that makes you qualified. This section should show employers that you can do the job. This should be treated just like your Experience section. Make sure that you include more than just the name of your school and your major. You should use bullet points and add more information when it makes sense. Only include your GPA if it's above a 3.0. I also suggest that you get more LinkedIn Licenses & Certifications which will show on your profile. LinkedIn bought Linda.com and merged it with LinkedIn Learning. When you take their online courses you will have the opportunity to add those certifications on your LinkedIn page. For example, if you are a marketing major and the companies that you're interested in want to see that you are good with Excel, you can actually take some Excel courses focused on marketing on LinkedIn Learning. You will earn badges by completing these courses or you can just write "proficient in Excel" as everyone else does. The example below is from a bright student, Briana Closs. Great job Briana!

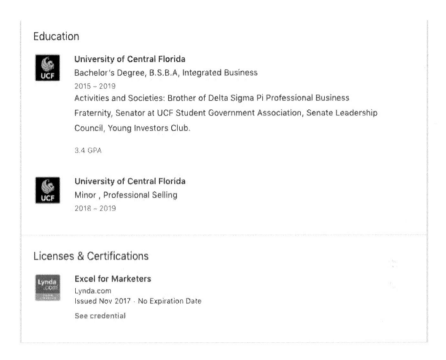

Education

University of Central Florida
Bachelor's Degree, B.S.B.A, Integrated Business
2015 – 2019
Activities and Societies: Brother of Delta Sigma Pi Professional Business
Fraternity, Senator at UCF Student Government Association, Senate Leadership
Council, Young Investors Club.

3.4 GPA

University of Central Florida
Minor , Professional Selling
2018 – 2019

Licenses & Certifications

Excel for Marketers
Lynda.com
Issued Nov 2017 · No Expiration Date
See credential

Just so you know, I follow my own advice. I'm not just telling you to do all of these things. When I left PepsiCo and worked in recruiting and talent acquisition, I wanted to let my customers know that I was proficient in this area so that they would see me as a subject matter expert. In order to do this, I took courses and added these badges on my LinkedIn.

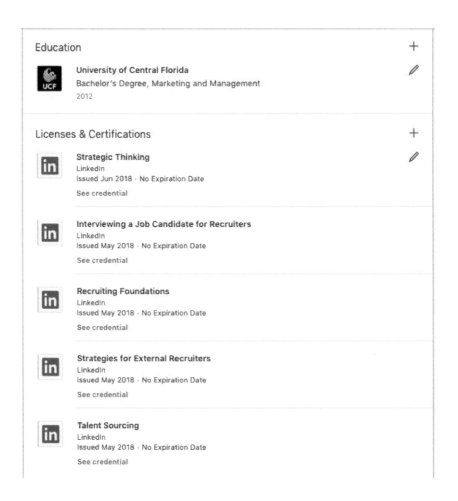

Education   +

University of Central Florida ✎
Bachelor's Degree, Marketing and Management
2012

Licenses & Certifications   +

Strategic Thinking ✎
LinkedIn
Issued Jun 2018 · No Expiration Date
See credential

Interviewing a Job Candidate for Recruiters
LinkedIn
Issued May 2018 · No Expiration Date
See credential

Recruiting Foundations
LinkedIn
Issued May 2018 · No Expiration Date
See credential

Strategies for External Recruiters
LinkedIn
Issued May 2018 · No Expiration Date
See credential

Talent Sourcing
LinkedIn
Issued May 2018 · No Expiration Date
See credential

Volunteer Experience

The next section is Volunteer Experience. In this section, you should talk about what the organization does and provide bullet points highlighting what you have been able to accomplish there.

I will again show Karla Santiago's profile since she has done a good job writing this section. This is a section that a lot of people tend to overlook.

Volunteer Experience

Public Speaking Volunteer
UCF - Puerto Rican Student Association
Sep 2018 • 1 mo
Disaster and Humanitarian Relief

• Spoke on behalf of the displaced Puerto Rican students affected by Hurricane Maria in order to advocate for an extension of our in-state tuition waiver.
• Assisted in getting the extension approved, which generated over $60,000 of financial aid for upwards of 300 students.
• Created and presented a transfer credit equivalency seminar for 50 Puerto Rican undergraduate students.

Service Project Volunteer
Boy Scouts of America
Nov 2017 • 1 mo
Social Services

Helped coordinate and manage a service project for a BSA Venturing Crew Member for Annabell's Closet, a Florida Based non-profit organization that gives resources to women coming out of abusive relationships.

Pavillion Volunteer
Ricky Martin Foundation
Jan 2013 – May 2015 • 2 yrs 5 mos
Civil Rights and Social Action

Worked as a Pavillion volunteer where we would motivate passerby's to learn more about the human trafficking epidemic going on in the world. We would also instruct them on how their donations or contributions by purchasing the foundation's merchandise would make a difference to the investigation of this cause.

Beach Clean Up Participant
Scuba Dogs
Aug 2013 – May 2014 • 10 mos
Environment

Participated in multiple beach clean ups around Puerto Rico.

Skills & Endorsements And Recommendations

I'm going to cover the next two sections together which are Skills & Endorsements and Recommendations. These sections allow you to build on your social proof. They will help you gain credibility and help you stand out. These sections work just like reviews for restaurants. You should be consciously making an effort to ask for recommendations to help build your social proof. You should also give recommendations when they are deserved. I have included a screenshot of my page as an example. As you can see, it just adds a whole new level of social proof and validity to my profile. It helps to back up everything I said above this section and it shows that I am a credible person.

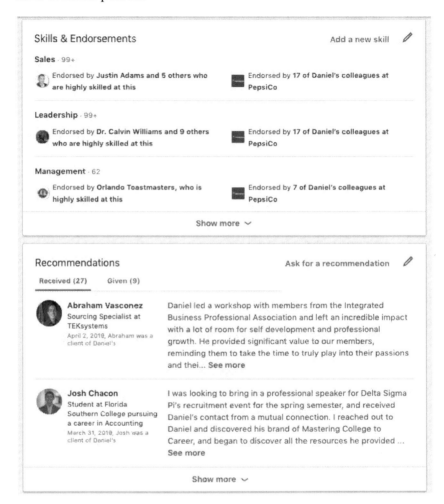

Accomplishments And Interest

The last two sections are Accomplishments and Interests. The Accomplishment section should list awards and honors that you have received throughout the years. This could include scholarships for example. The Interests section shows companies or people you follow on LinkedIn. I would suggest that you follow all of the companies on your target list. This will give you an edge when recruiters from companies on your target list are looking at your profile. It helps to show that you are interested in working for their company. It will also give the recruiters an idea of the other things that you are passionate about. I've included an example from Chad White's profile so you can see how he did a nice job adding his courses, his awards, and following companies that he is interested in working for. Great job Chad!

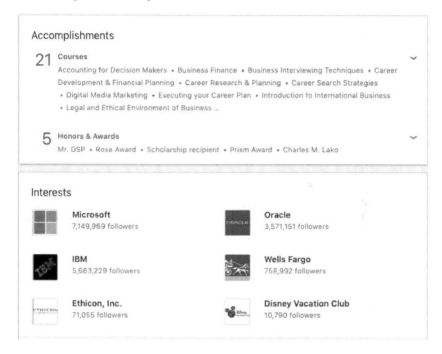

Student All-Star Example

I've shown you bits and pieces of LinkedIn profiles and now i'm going to show you a complete profile. This is Jessica Lupo's LinkedIn profile and she's done an amazing job with it.

She has a professional headshot and a banner that shares more about her. Her summary could go into more detail but it still works. It's short and to the point.

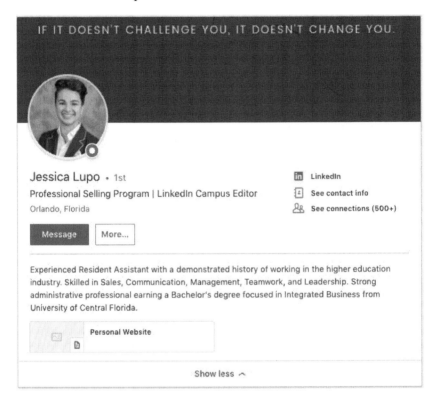

She does a very good job sharing her experience. She included the jobs that she's held, her experience at school as a member of the Professional Selling Program and as a Resident Assistant, her internship experience, etc.

Experience

Campus Editor

LinkedIn

Dec 2018 – Present · 5 mos

• Chosen as one of 630 students from 500 colleges across 40 countries to help mobilize peers to publish what matters to them utilizing LinkedIn
• Representing the University of Central Florida and acting as a LinkedIn ambassador to build awareness and showcase the power of LinkedIn
• Overall goal to produce quality content such as published articles on LinkedIn, creative videos or meaningful posts to meet monthly goals

 LinkedIn Campus Editor

University of Central Florida

1 yr 5 mos

Professional Selling Program Member
Nov 2018 – Present · 6 mos
Orlando, Florida Area

The Professional Selling Program is a prestigious, specialized program offered by the Department of Marketing at the University of Central Florida. The nationally recognized program accepts no more than 35 applicants of the 70,000+ enrolled at the University of Central Florida and is one of only approximately 120 specialized sales undergradua... See more

 Spring 2019 Cohort Professional Sellin...   **Professional Selling Program Acceptan...**

Resident Assistant
Dec 2017 – Present · 1 yr 5 mos
Orlando, Florida

• Marketed student centered university programs to promote diversity, emotional, social, and educational understanding and growth
• Created and maintained a positive living environment designed to link community, faculty, and residents, often resolving conflict... See more

Participant

Liberty Mutual Insurance

Oct 2018 · 1 mo
Greater Boston Area

 Photo at the Student Diversity Symposium

145

Summer Analyst - Private Wealth Management

Goldman Sachs

May 2018 – Aug 2018 · 4 mos
Jersey City, New Jersey

• Worked within Investment Management Division Corporate Controllers as a Private Wealth Management Summer Analyst
• Preformed daily, weekly, and monthly data analysis related to Incentive Fees reporting by the Private Wealth Management team... See more

INROADS Finance Intern

UTC Aerospace Systems

Jun 2017 – Aug 2017 · 3 mos
Miramar, Florida

• Performed data testing in accordance with Sarbanes-Oxley requirements to certify proper authorization and timely processing
• Worked directly with the International Air Transport Association Controller to reduce energy costs throughout UTC. Analyzed past electricity expenses and proposed usage mo...
See more

Show 1 more experience ⌄

Education

University of Central Florida

Bachelor's degree, Integrated Business

2017 – 2020

Activities and Societies: I-Corps, Delta Sigma Pi, Collegiate DECA

Broward College

Associate of Arts (A.A.), Accounting and Business/Management

2015 – 2017

Activities and Societies: Phi Beta Lambda Community Service Vice President, Phi Theta Kappa Financial Ambassador, Honor Student Committee, Student Government Committee, and Student Global Organization.

Look at the number of Licenses & Certifications Jessica has. They show her vast array of knowledge with credible companies like Bloomberg and Google.

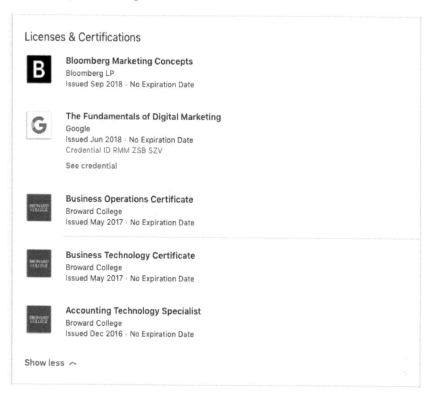

She again does a great job sharing her Volunteer Experience not only detailing what the organizations are about, but also explaining her role with them.

Volunteer Experience

Project Coordinator
Be The Match operated by National Marrow Donor Program
Nov 2016 • 1 mo
Health

Served as team lead for a group of 30 volunteers during an on-campus cheek swabbing event for bone marrow transplants. Our mission was to swab cheeks, register donors, and increase the pool of ethnically diverse people that are underrepresented in the bone marrow registry. Our Phi Beta Lambda (PBL) chapter challenged Broward College's student and faculty to "Knock Out Cancer!" PBL members collaborated with Be The Match, who is operated under the National Marrow Donor Program which manages the largest and most diverse bone marrow registry in the world, to plan multiple swabbing events. Together we registered 82 potentially lifesaving donors into the bone marrow registry.

Student Ambassador & Team Captain
American Cancer Society
Apr 2016 • 1 mo
Health

Our mission as a chapter since day one was to raise over $1500.00 for Relay and we did just that. At the event itself our NHS booth featured a donated dunk tank, cupcakes, and glow in the dark bracelets for the Luminaria walk. The dunk tank featured NHS Members, the NHS Sponsor, and the NHS President, all ready for the drop into the cold water below them. For $1.00 everyone had 2 chances for the dunk tank. Members during the event volunteers their time by selling merchandise in the booth, setting up recycle bins around the track for bottles and cans, and staying from 4pm until 8am the next morning because cancer never sleeps. All the proceeds from our booth benefited the American Cancer Society. Members were able to decorate Luminaria bags for cancer victims and donate canned goods used to hold down the bags. These cans are later donated to local food banks. Blankets were handmade by members to be donated to an organization that distributes them to hospital centers. Purple cancer ribbons were also created, decorated, and sold at the 3v3 basketball tournament in order to raise more money for the team. NHS Members also helped out a local Relay team known as "Hunting for a Cure" with making blankets. As NHS Chapter President, Team Captain, and Relay for Life committee Student Ambassador, I pushed my chapter to work harder than ever before. Planning since June we were able to have the most interactive and creative booth at Relay for Life. Meeting our goal as a chapter was rewarding and showed members the difference they made to not only the chapter, but to local families and cancer survivors.

In her Skills & Endorsements and Recommendations sections she has some social proof, but she could definitely work on getting more. Even with what she has, it allows employers to know that what she has stated in her profile is real.

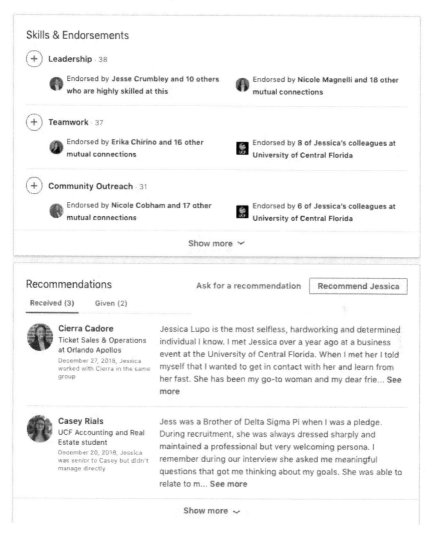

In the Accomplishments and Interests sections, Jessica again does a great job sharing what she has done and what she is interested in.

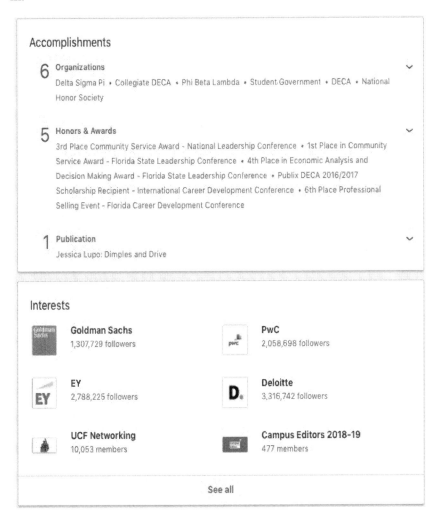

Accomplishments

6 Organizations

Delta Sigma Pi • Collegiate DECA • Phi Beta Lambda • Student Government • DECA • National Honor Society

5 Honors & Awards

3rd Place Community Service Award - National Leadership Conference • 1st Place in Community Service Award - Florida State Leadership Conference • 4th Place in Economic Analysis and Decision Making Award - Florida State Leadership Conference • Publix DECA 2016/2017 Scholarship Recipient - International Career Development Conference • 6th Place Professional Selling Event - Florida Career Development Conference

1 Publication

Jessica Lupo: Dimples and Drive

Interests

Goldman Sachs
1,307,729 followers

PwC
2,058,698 followers

EY
2,788,225 followers

Deloitte
3,316,742 followers

UCF Networking
10,053 members

Campus Editors 2018-19
477 members

See all

Overall, Jessica has done an outstanding job letting anybody who reads her profile know what her accomplishments are, what she wants to do in the future, and why she would be a great candidate. She does an amazing job going above and beyond and making her profile stand out among the crowd.

Creating Content For Linkedin

After you've created an all-star profile, it's time to take it one step further. I want you to stand out among the crowd by engaging and posting on LinkedIn. By engaging in other peoples' posts and by posting content of your own, you will be able to attract people to look at your page. The point of creating that amazing LinkedIn profile is for people to look at it after all!

You don't just want to post content to get engagement, you want to post content to build your personal brand. Be authentic and let your personality show. By being yourself you will attract companies, recruiters, and people who want to work with you based on who you are. There is no need to try to be like someone else or to be serious and uptight on LinkedIn. I understand that LinkedIn is supposed to be professional, but you can still be professional being yourself.

Now I'll go over some of my favorite ways that students can create content and stand out.

Reposting Other People's Content

Reposting people's content is a simple way to post because you're not doing the heavy lifting of creating the content. Instead, you're sharing your thoughts on the content. Just make sure that you give credit to the account that originally posted the content. Here is an example of an article that Karla Santiago shared because she's passionate about the topic. It does not need to be complicated, you just need to post.

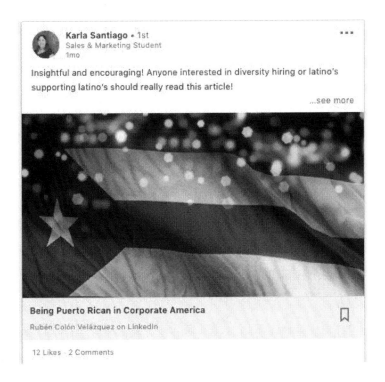

Sharing Your Wins

Another great type of post is sharing your wins. They can be as big as sharing that you accepted an internship with Microsoft or something as small as sharing that you got a good grade on a test. This may sound like bragging, but look at it more like social proof. I would not do it every single day, but once every couple of weeks helps to build your brand. You can also add the hashtag #humblebrag to make it seem less like you're bragging. Here is an example of a post from Jessica Lupo.

Jessica Lupo • 1st

Professional Selling Program | LinkedIn Campus Editor

22h

• • •

I am humbled to announce that this summer I will be joining the Microsoft team in Washington as a Finance Rotation Program Intern! Words cannot express how excited and grateful I am for this opportunity.

A huge thank you to everyone who has played a part in my professional growth and development. I wouldn't be where I am without you!

This summer I will be starting a podcast and documenting my progress on LinkedIn using #LupoLearning. Stay tuned!

#Summer2019 #Microsoft #LupoLearning

116 Likes · 34 Comments

 Like ☐ Comment ↪ Share

Sharing Learning Lessons

Another great post for college students is sharing something that you learned that really stuck out to you. This is a great way to show employers that you understand what you are learning in class and that you value your education. I love how in the next example, Grant Smith does such a good job taking something he learned in an improv session and sharing how that same lesson also applies to business. Great Job Grant!

Grant Smith • 1st

Marketing Student | Head of Social Media of AMA at UCF | College of B...

1mo

"No scene is ever about the words being spoken" -Del Close.

This was a lesson from one of our improv sessions. However, I thought that one can also find meaning in this quote in the workplace as well. Whether it's simple office politics or presenting a new #marketing plan for the #company, there is always more going on in the background than what the situation might entail.

That workplace drama may be the result of a small frustration in #accounting. While that marketing proposal would truly help the business thrive, the general #manager is thinking about the costs to implement such a plan.

Context is important. The relationships and actions that take place now truly matter in what happens next in the #business scene.

1 Like · 1 Comment

Posting A Video

The last type of post that I will share with you is creating a video of yourself and posting it on LinkedIn. This type of post will require the most work, but it will generally give you the best results. These videos can be about an experience that you had, a lesson that you learned, a recent win, or anything else you may want to talk about. Videos are great because they allow others to get to know you on a different level. In the below example, Luis Guzman talked about interviewing in a quick 30-second video. I want you to take an extra close look at the level of engagement. Almost 4,000 views! Now that is great awareness for your personal brand.

Engaging With Other People's Posts

At this point, you should have your LinkedIn profile completed and you should have started to post content. The next step is to engage with others. Connect and engage with other students, faculty, the individuals you selected on your 10-5-1 activity, and anyone else you find interesting. This should be a daily habit. One piece of advice that I like to give students is for them to comment on at least ten posts each day. This helps establish yourself in the community and it helps you to stand out and grow your personal brand.

By now you have all of the tools to be a LinkedIn expert as a student. LinkedIn is one of the best tools out there for students to use. There is not a more important social media platform for college students than LinkedIn. The best thing is that LinkedIn is where Instagram was five to eight years ago, meaning that there is a lot of opportunity to be seen if you are active on the platform.

Not many people are posting content themselves so people's feeds aren't too cluttered yet. When you post something on Instagram or Facebook now, less than 10% of your friends will see it unless it gets above average engagement. Only then will the algorithm share your post with more people. Your posts on LinkedIn will be seen by the majority of your connections on the other hand. In fact, when someone likes or comments on your post it will show on their connections feeds too. Get on the LinkedIn train before it gets too saturated and it's too late!

MY GIFT TO YOU!

Free Access to the LinkedIn Lessons Of My Online Program

I have seen a significant correlation between the types of jobs that students who are active on LinkedIn receive versus the jobs that students who are not active on LinkedIn receive. This is why I have dedicated one of the lessons included in the mini course to this topic are the two on LinkedIn

Enjoy,

Daniel

Or visit http://bit.ly/mc2cminicourse

CHAPTER 14
TALKING TO EMPLOYERS

Approaching The Employer

After all this work that you've done, it's time to start approaching employers. Again, you want to make sure that you stand out and that you make good first impressions. You never get a second chance to make a first impression.

Remember that most recruiters are afraid to make a bad hire. A bad hire will cost them one to three-times that person's first-year salary so taking the time to understand their wants and needs will be crucial for us understanding what to say in our first encounter. By now you should have a lot of this information. This information should have been gathered when you were looking for the answers to your open book test. This information includes the qualities and traits that they are looking for in their ideal candidate. What positions are they hiring for and how many people are they looking to hire for that role? What are the company's value and mission statement? Knowing this information, you want to let them know what you have done to prepare for this position.

Find out if the companies on your target list are scheduled to be on campus at any point. They may be on campus for career fair, mock interviews, information sessions, workshops, etc. Once you have found out when they will be on campus it is crucial that you attend the event. Get there early and sit in the front row. Also, don't forget to ask insightful questions.

Before the day of the event, make sure that you are engaging with the employer. Comment and like their posts on LinkedIn. If they post something promoting the event, make sure you share it and even comment to let them know that you are excited about the event and look forward to meeting them. The goal here is to have them notice you and already be looking for you at the event. This shows them a whole different level of interest and commitment.

If your target companies aren't scheduled to visit your school, don't be upset. I think this gives you a great opportunity to try and get them to come. There are a couple of ways for you to do this. One way is to partner with the employer relations department. You can work with them and they can help you contact them as I explained earlier in the book. A second way is for you to bring them on campus yourself. You can ask them if they would be interested in speaking to a student organization that you're involved with. Let them know that there are many students like you who would love to learn more about the job opportunities they offer. Let them know that you would be more than happy to set up the event and market it around campus. All they would have to do is come and speak about themselves and the company. Some of you may be wondering why you would bring the company to talk to other students because it would be creating competition for you. I don't think this is the case at all. I think the fact that you set it all up already sets you apart and shows the company that you are a leader and a self-starter.

I am going to share with you a secret tactic to talk to an employer that you want to work for. I call this the resume critique. This concept works for both resumes and interviews. The point here is to reach out to the recruiter of the company you want to work for and ask them to critique your resume. Please remember that you need to build some sort of relationship with them before you ask this favor. By asking them to do this they will look at your resume in detail. The great thing about this tactic is that you minimize the risk of them not liking your resume because they've given you advice. There is also a chance that they could like your resume and bring you in for an interview. Just think about it. They could look at the resume in detail and give you advice on how to fix your resume to their liking. This is great, but what if your resume is already perfect? Then you are making a great impression and you still win! This also works the same way for interviews. You could ask the recruiter if they would do a short mock interview with you. Again, they will give you feedback on what you need to work on, but if you kill the interview they will want to schedule you for a real interview. The best part is that you now know what to expect from the interview. This is what I like to call a low-risk with high-reward tactic!

Mastering The Career Fair

One of my favorite episodes of the podcast was when I had the opportunity to interview one of my mentors, Dr. Calvin Williams. He served as the Associate Director of Employer Relations at the University of Central Florida and as Director of Employer Relations at Florida State University. Employer relations is the department responsible for hosting and preparing the career fairs and expos at colleges and universities. Dr. William gave a lot of great insight that I will be sharing with you.

One thing that he told me was that students should see their school's career fair as the Super Bowl. You need to consider it to be the most important day of the semester. It's not every day that you have hundreds of companies looking to hire college students in one place. Make sure you take it seriously and follow the advice I am going to share with you. If you follow the advice, don't be surprised if you walk away from career fair with a couple of interviews already lined up.

When walking into a career fair you need to have a plan. The plan starts with doing some research to see which companies will be in attendance and understanding what roles they are there to hire. When I worked for PepsiCo and we attended career fairs we only hired for sales and operations roles. When students were looking for information about our marketing positions we sent them to our website. Understanding what the companies are there to hire for is important. All of this information can be found on your school's career services website. Depending on the size of the career fair you could have hundreds of companies in attendance. When conducting the research I want you to create a target list based on the companies that will be in attendance. Make sure you keep it below ten companies. This will allow you to focus and it will give you more time to get familiar with each company. I want you to create custom resumes and cover letters for each of your target companies understanding what they are hiring for and who will be there representing the company. I also want you to find out if the company is local or if they are traveling to attend the event. I will explain the importance of this later on. One other thing that you need to make sure that you do is dress professionally. Make sure your suit is ironed and that your shoes are clean.

The day has come and you are now entering the building. Now what? First, walk around and make yourself familiar with the venue. Locate where your target companies are and then start talking to companies that are not on your target list first. Yes, you heard me right. Talk to companies that aren't on your target list first. This is important because you will naturally be nervous and I want you to warm up talking to companies that you're not interested in. That way if you stumble and mess up it doesn't matter. Once you have warmed up and you've got your pitch perfected it's time to approach your target companies.

From my time as an employer at career fairs talking to students, I realized that most students had no clue what we were hiring for. Even worse, they had no idea what we look for in our future employees. I would say that nine out of ten students who approached me would start by introducing themselves and then ask what I was hiring for. That generally meant they were going straight into the no pile. Don't worry, because you have already done this research you will be prepared. During your conversation with the recruiters make sure you let them know that you did your research and that you know what they're hiring for. This will definitely help you stand out. Imagine that you are the recruiter for a moment and a student came up to you and said the following:

"Hi Mr. Botero, My name is Daniel and I am very excited to have the pleasure to be speaking with you today. I know that PepsiCo is a great company because they care about the communities they do business in. They have led growth for all Fortune 500 CPG companies for the past five years, and have a great sales associate program. From my research and talking to employees that have gone through the sales associate program I know that you are looking for students who have great work ethic, good communication skills, and good leadership skills. I believe I would make a great candidate for this role because on top of being a full-time student I am the president of my student organization, I have done an internship in sales, and I work four nights a week as a server to pay for school. I would love to give you a copy of my resume and cover letter that I created just for PepsiCo and the sales associate position."

Would you not put their resume in the yes pile and schedule this person for an interview?

This is exactly what I want you to do with all your target companies. For the companies that traveled into town for the career expo, I want you to ask for the interview. These companies work with career services to reserve rooms on campus to conduct initial interviews. They don't want to have to travel back so they come to campus and stay for a couple of days. You can find this information on the career services website or by going into career services and asking them yourself. If you know that is the case I want you to make sure you ask for the interview.

Make sure you ask for business cards for every employer you meet. If they don't have it connect with them on LinkedIn right away. Like I talked about in the networking chapter, follow-up is key. Make sure you have sent a follow-up email and a handwritten thank you card in the first twenty-four hours.

CHAPTER 15

MASTERING THE RESUME

S tudents are always trying to create the best resume. They feel that their resume will be the reason why they will land their dream job. Yes, your resume is important and you should have a well-written resume with no grammar or spelling errors. It should be easy to read and you should be able to look at it in fifteen seconds and be able to understand it. The reality is that I could write a whole book teaching you how to write a good resume. In fact, there are hundreds of books out there already that can teach you on this topic. You also have tons of free resources as a student to help you build the perfect resume. One of the services that every career services department offers is resume writing support. This is why I'm not going to focus on the basics of resume writing. Instead, I am going to go over what career services does not teach you.

What Is A Resume?

Have you ever really thought about what a resume is? I have come to the conclusion that a resume is the most biased document in the world. You spend countless hours creating a one to two-page document that talks about all of the great things about you and none of the bad. On top of that, people tend to lie or exaggerate on their resumes. This makes recruiters a little skeptical when reviewing them. Because of this, recruiters take what's written on a resume with a grain of salt. It's your job to prove to them that your resume is not made up and that you actually have done everything that you said you did on that piece of paper. This is why I always say that who you hand your resume to is more important than what's on your actual resume. You could have the best resume in the world and you could also be the most qualified, but all of that won't matter if your resume is not given a fair shot.

Let's talk about a made-up scenario of two students. One student's name is Paula and the other student is named Ryan. They are both interested in working at Target for their management training program. Paula is more qualified and has a perfectly written resume. She worked with her professors and career services department to make sure her resume was perfect. She logs onto Handshake or whatever platform your university uses to post jobs available to the students and applies for the job with Target. She submitted her perfect resume online and she now sits and waits to see what happens. Ryan too has a resume, but his resume is not as strong as Paula's. Ryan meets the basic qualifications for this job. Instead of applying online, he was able to get one of his mentors to email his resume to Jenn, the person in charge of hiring for this particular role. Ryan's mentor even writes a short note explaining why he thinks Ryan would be a good fit for the position.

Now let's put ourselves in Jenn's situation. She is a very busy person. She probably has a lot on her plate like most people working in corporate America. She has a goal of hiring at least twenty people each year for this role alone. She checks the applications and she sees that seven-hundred students have submitted their resumes for this position. She does not have time to read every word on each of those seven-hundred resumes. That would take weeks. She uses her ATS (applicant tracking system) to pull out resumes that match what she is looking for. This helps Jenn go from seven-hundred to three-hundred and fifty resumes. The ATS was able to cut the resume pile in half.

At this point, we will assume that since Paula had a well written resume and she created a custom resume for Target that her resume made the cut. Ryan's resume will bypass this step since his resume was not in the original pile of seven-hundred students, but it's in Jenn's email. Now Jenn has three-hundred and fifty resumes that she needs to review. Three-hundred and fifty resumes is still a lot of resumes so she does what most people in her shoes would do. She skims through the resumes. In fact, the average recruiter spends less than six seconds reading a resume. And yes, this is the same resume that you have spent countless hours creating. In those six seconds that Jenn is skimming a resume she is trying to determine whether the resume will go in to one of three piles.There's the yes pile, the no pile, and the maybe pile. By the time she is done skimming the resumes she has one-hundred and fifty in the no pile, seventy-five in the maybe pile, and seventy-five in the yes pile. Paula's perfect resume again made it through the cut and she is now one of seventy-five students in the yes pile. Ryan's resume is still in Jenn's email inbox. Now Jenn takes no more than six seconds to review the resumes in the yes pile. She narrows it down to twenty-five students, including Paula, whom she likes and invites to interview. Paula's resume made it to the finish line. It was able to pass the ATS, the six second review, and the final readthrough. That is a lot of steps to have to get through just to be fully reviewed by Jenn. But, let's face it, it's hard to create the perfect resume especially because your resume can be interpreted differently depending on who is reading it. This is why no matter how many times you have gotten your resume reviewed you will always get different feedback. Now, let's go back to Ryan. Remember, his resume was sent directly to Jenn by one of his mentors. Because Jenn has a relationship with his mentor and there is a level of trust and respect, Jenn opens the email and immediately fully reviews Ryan's resume in detail. Wait, what? Ryan did not take as much time creating his resume. The reason why Jenn read Ryan's resume immediately is because it's no longer the most biased document in the world. Ryan's resume is as good as the relationship that Ryan's mentor and Jenn have.

The reality is that Ryan's story is not really a made up scenario. Ryan was one of the students that I mentored and I actually sent his resume to Jenn. Jenn saw the resume and reached out to Ryan within a week. Ryan had a phone call with Jenn which lead to an interview. Paula was a person I made up, but she represents all the students who focus solely on the resume and not on making sure you hand your resume to the right person. Handing your resume is so important and most people don't focus on this. Even in Paula's scenario, I had her pass all the cuts, but what about the other students who didn't?

Long story short, our resume is important, but who you hand your resume to is more important.

Catering To Two Audiences

Ideally, you always want to have someone act as your sponsor and send your resume to the decision maker, but the reality is that this is not always possible. So how do you ensure that your resume makes it past all of the cuts? Again, I'm not focusing on the basic resume structure. I'm focusing on expert level strategies that will help your resume stand out and get read.

Nowadays having a beautiful resume that is appealing to the human eye is not enough. The reality is that companies are always looking for efficiency and they're finding ways to automate as much as possible. In the above example, I said that there were seven-hundred applicants. The reason that I used that number is because that is the average number of candidates who apply for each open role online. Companies use applicant tracking systems (ATS) to keep track of the hundreds of applicants and to filter applications using specific search criteria in order to save time and resources. To give you a better idea of what an ATS actually is I'll give you

Wikipedia's definition.

"An applicant tracking system (ATS) is a software application that enables the electronic handling of recruitment needs. An ATS can be implemented or accessed online on an enterprise or small business level, depending on the needs of the company and there is also free and open source ATS software available. An ATS is very similar to customer relationship management (CRM) systems, but are designed for recruitment tracking purposes. In many cases, they filter applications automatically based on given criteria such as keywords, skills, former employers, years of experience and schools attended. This has caused many to adapt resume optimization techniques similar to those used in search engine optimization when creating and formatting their résumé."

As you can tell from this definition, you need to make sure your resume is also designed for the ATS. You need to use the keywords that the companies you are applying for are looking for. The old way of having one resume and using it to apply to every company is long gone. You need to make sure you have custom resumes for each role you are interested in. This is a big reason why having the sniper approach that we spoke about earlier in the book is crucial to your job search.

Many of the free resources out there used to help students create resumes don't take the ATS into account. They are great for building a basic resume, but they fail to ensure that your resume is keyword optimized. This is why I highly encourage you to work with a professional resume writer. I personally don't provide this service but I have a couple of people whom I trust that I would recommend you to use. Visit Masteringcollegetocareer.com/resources if you're interested in getting more information.

The goal of the resume is to get you an interview so let's move onto that topic. It is in the interview that you close the deal!

CHAPTER 16
MASTERING THE INTERVIEW

C ongratulations, all the work that you have done so far has landed you the interview. This is your chance to impress your dream company, so you need to be ready. In this chapter, we will cover some basic interview techniques. We will focus on the strategy of interviewing. It's important that you understand the mind of the interviewer. You need to overcome their objections to make them feel like the decision to extend you a job offer is a no brainer.

I will break down the interview into three sections. We will talk about what happens before the interview, during the interview, and after the interview. Each step is crucial and not taking one of these steps seriously will lower your chances of getting the job. The last thing that I want is for you to get this far, only to get this far. We are almost at the finish line so let's cross it!

Before The Interview

Congratulations! You received the email and your interview is set. It is time to get ready. The first thing that you need to do is more research. You need to make sure that you're prepared. You want to make sure that you are familiar with the company, the role, and the individuals interviewing you.

Let's start with the information that you need to know before the interview. You should know what the company is about, their mission and vision statements, their goals, and where they see the company five years down the line. You also need to understand how the company makes money. Understanding how revenue is generated is crucial. Regardless of the position, you are either selling or facilitating the sales of the companies products and services. You also want to understand the competitive landscape. Who are the main competitors and what makes them different? If you are interviewing with a publicly traded company all of this information is much easier to find. A lot of this information can be found in the company's annual report.

The second thing you want to do a lot of research on is the role that you're interviewing for. I encourage you to visit websites like Glassdoor.com to see what people who held that position say about it. You will also be able to find out compensation and much more information. You should know the goal of the role so that you can figure out how you're solving a need for the organization. How many people in the company have the same role? What roles do people who do a great job in that position move into next? Try to understand what a typical week looks like. In most entry-level jobs you spend 80% of your time working on 20% of the tasks in the job description. Try to understand what these tasks are. Try to picture yourself in the role. What areas will you exceed in and what areas do you think you will struggle with? Go on LinkedIn and try to connect with people who are currently in that role or were in that role. They will be the best resource to get this information. You can reach out to them, let them know that you have an interview coming up, and ask them about their experience. You should already know a lot of this information when you did your research during your self-assessment. If you don't know the answers to these questions, don't worry it's not too late.

Last but not least, do your homework on the interviewer. Who are you interviewing with and what is their role? The way that a recruiter or human resource employee would interview is

172

completely different than how your potential manager would interview you. Different people will be looking for different things. You need to be prepared to adjust your answers and your examples to overcome their personal objections. What you will find is that the bigger the role and the bigger the investment from the company, the more interviews you will have. This is due to the fact that a bad hire costs one to three-times the first year salary for that position. The company will use more resources in the interview process to lower their risk of a bad hire.

When I went through the interviewing process with PepsiCo I interviewed with HR, my reporting manager, and the regional vice president. The first interview is usually with someone on the talent acquisition or human resource team. In general, they are looking to make sure that you are qualified for the job. They are going to be more focused on making sure you have the right experience to be successful at the job. They will spend most of the interview asking more structured questions and diving into your resume. Looking at this from their perspective they just want to make sure they are not hiring the wrong person. This is the HR departments biggest fear. For you, the goal of this interview should be to show them that you are qualified for the role and that you have the skills to be successful in the role. It comes down to you demonstrating to the interviewer that you have the answers to their open book test. This will move you along to the next round. Once you pass this test, you will have gained an ally. It is now in the HR employees best interest to help you get the job. This is because they have already given you their blessing since they pushed you through to the next round. Take advantage of that and reach back out to them to ask for advice on how to prepare for the next interview. If you do well in the interview it will make the HR employee look good because it shows that they're doing a good job at finding top talent.

I mentioned that my second interview was with the person who would be my direct manager. This person's concern is not as much about whether you can do the job or not. It is more about if they think you would be a good fit for the team. He or she will most likely assume that you're qualified to do the job since HR already pushed you through. The focus of this interview would most likely be more about personality. Your goal before coming into this type of interview should be to learn about this managers leadership style and you should also try to connect with individuals on the team. Remember, people hire people they like and trust. If you can prove that you will be a good fit for the team, you will move onto the final interview with that person's boss.

Congratulations, you have made it to the final interview! To be successful in this interview you need to think big picture. The more senior the person you are meeting with, the more big picture they are thinking. They are probably looking for potential in this interview. They trust that you can do the job that you're interviewing for otherwise you would not have made it this far. This person will be analyzing whether or not they think you will excel and if you could do the job that is two positions above the one you're interviewing for. He or she also wants to make sure that you're going to stick around and that they can see you staying with the company for at least two years. Again, they think big picture and they understand the investment that comes from a bad hire. You will want to make sure that this person can tell that you've spent a considerable amount of time researching the company and that you're really interested in the position. This is usually the last interview that you will have, but it all depends on the organization. The bigger the role that you are interviewing for, the more steps and the more people you will interview with.

In addition to all of the research that you need to do, you also need to dress professionally for the interview. It is better that you are overdressed than underdressed. Be sure to bring a couple of extra resumes, your career portfolio that we talked about earlier, and a pen and paper to take notes. There should be absolutely no note taking on your phone or any other electronic device.

The last thing that I want you to do before the interview is to come up with questions that you will ask. At the end of every interview, you will be asked if you have any questions. Never leave an interview without asking questions. Make sure these are good questions. These should not be questions that you can find the answers to easily by Googling them. If anything, it's better to ask questions about the interviewers personal experience with the company than to ask generic questions.

Now that you've done all you can to prepare, it's interview time!

During The Interview

The big day has arrived and you are prepared. Go into the interview with confidence, but make sure you are not cocky. There is a fine line, but confidence during an interview is key.

Most interviews will follow a similar process. You are welcomed to the interview, then you will jump into some sort of small talk, and then they'll ask you about your resume. Each company will have a slightly different way of interviewing, but you should know what you are walking into through the research that you conducted in the pre-interview steps.

It is important that you are able to talk about yourself and that you're able to walk someone through your resume. From there you will most likely be asked a series of behavioral questions. The goal of asking behavioral questions is to assess the candidate's past experience to see if they will be able to do the job they are interviewing for. Past performance is the best indicator of future performance. The way that you answer these questions will allow the interviewer to get an idea as to how you would handle similar situations in that role. An example of this type of question is, "Tell me about a time when you had to work in a group with difficult people." They basically want to know what you were working on, how you handled the situation, and what ultimately happened. To answer these types of questions I suggest that you use the STAR method.

The STAR method is a formatted way to answer behavioral questions and stands for Situation, Task, Action, Results.

Situation - Explain the situation.

Task - Describe the task at hand. What is the challenge that you were facing and what needed to be done?

Action - Elaborate on the specific actions that you took to complete the task.

Results - Explain the results. What was the final outcome? What did you accomplish? Quantifying your results is always best. You can explain how much you sold or saved the company for example.

Don't be afraid to take a few seconds to think about your response. You don't want there to be an awkward silence, but it's best to take a few seconds to compose your thoughts so that you don't end up rambling.

Once they have asked you all of their questions they will turn it over to you to see if you have any questions. Like I mentioned before, ask them questions. It not only shows that you are interested in the position, but it also shows that you are interviewing them just as much as they are interviewing you. Choose questions that you cannot find the answers online for.

Pro Tip: Don't ask questions about compensation in the first interview. Make sure you research that online so you have an idea of what the salary would be. If they ask you what you are looking to make, always answer with a range. For example, if you research a position and the average person makes $50,000 you can say that you're looking to make between $50,000 to $60,000. This will allow you to not get locked into a number later on and it will help with any future negotiations.

Regardless of what questions you decide to ask, I recommend asking a specific question for your final question. I truly believe that this question needs to be asked. You can change the wording around to make it work for you, but you need to make sure to ask it. The question is:

"Is there any particular reason why you think that I may not be a good fit for this position?"

This question gives you one last opportunity to overcome any objections that they may have about hiring you. Let's say that they are concerned that you may not be able to handle the long hours and the seasonality of the role. If you never ask this question, you could be denied the opportunity. This question also gives you the opportunity to get instant feedback from your interviewer. I see students walk away from interviews thinking they did great, but then are disappointed when they don't get the job. They are confused about why they were not asked to move forward in the interviewing process since they thought their interview went well. This question gives you a better idea of where you stand, allowing you to reassess your target list and move forward with the next best course of action.

Pro Tip: The Leave Behind

A leave behind is something that you leave for the interviewer. It is safe to say that less than 1% of students create leave-behinds. This little bit of extra effort will make you stand out. Your leave behind can be something creative and/or unique to the company or person you are interviewing with or it can be something as simple as items from your portfolio. I liked to make a personalized cover page with my name and the company's logo and include a copy of my personalized cover letter and resume. I would ask a couple of the individuals who wrote me letters of recommendation to adjust it to the company that I was interviewing with and I would add two to three more items from my portfolio that I think the interviewer would like to see. This makes for a simple, yet very impressive touch that is sure to make a lasting impression.

Here is an example of a few of the pages from the leave behind I made for my interviews with Frito Lay. If you would like to see the whole leave behind you can find it at MasteringCollegeTo Career.com/bookresources.

Daniel Botero's

Leave behind

Final Interviews with Frito Lay

April 11, 2012

Daniel Botero
7362 Spring Villas Cr.
Orlando, FL 32819
March 4, 2012

To Whom It May Concern,

As a senior in college and a proud member of the UCF Professional Selling Program, I believe that I am very well suited for the Sales Associate role with Frito Lay. I have acquired more than an adamant amount of experience in sales and leadership. I have also obtained a level of customer service and education that would allow me to perform the requirements of this position efficiently. Some reasons why I believe that I am a competitive candidate for this position are as follows:

- I am currently acquiring a double major in Marketing with a Professional Selling track and Entrepreneurship Management. I also work part time and hold a leadership position with the Delta Sigma Pi professional organization. This demonstrates my willingness to assume more than the typical level of responsibility, and to achieve in a challenging environment.

- Through my coursework and internships, I have acquired in-depth computer proficiency and a profound belief in the importance of effective communication in today's growing entrepreneurial environment.

- My employment with Universal Studios over the past five years has enabled me to learn and grow in many capacities. My ability to communicate and persuade effectively has made me an invaluable team member in the merchandize department and often recognized as a top performer.

As you can see, I am goal-oriented, driven, and not afraid of hard work. I believe that these qualifications are vital to anyone who would be a productive member of your organization, as I would like to be.

Best regards,

Daniel Botero
Professional Selling Program| Member
Majors| Marketing and Entrepreneurship
Delta Sigma Pi | Vice President of Professional Activities
Tutoring Matching Service | Director of Campus Operation
(C) 321-945-7270
Dbotero1@gmail.com

Daniel Botero

WWW.DanielBotero.Info ◆ (321) 945-7270 ◆ Dbotero1@Gmail.com ◆ 7362 Spring Villa Cir Orlando,FL

Language - Fluent in both English and Spanish

Education

University of Central Florida   Orlando, FL
Bachelor Science in Business Administration.   July 2012
Double Major: Marketing with a Professional Selling track and Management with an Entrepreneurship track

Scholarships
Florida Bright Future ◆ Scholarship America ◆ VCC Road Map to Success ◆ J.C Aspley Scholarship ◆ Disney's Dreamer and Doer
Competitions and Awards
Finalist-UCF King of the Court Bus. Plan Com. ◆ Semi-Finalist-UCF Joust Bus Plan Com. ◆ 3rd --DECA Entrepreneurship Com.
Academic Organizations
Professional Selling Program - *Member*   Orlando,FL-Aug. 2011 - Present
   ◆ Only 30 students out of more than 5000 business students are accepted a year
   ◆ Corporate partners consider it to be equivalent to one to two years of professional sales experience
   ◆ Mentee with a Sr. Account Manager of Enterprise Rent-A-Car and District Sales Manager of SRS Medical
   ◆ Rated one of the best sales programs in the nation by the University Sales Education Foundation
Delta Sigma Pi - Professional Organization - *VP of Professional Activities*   Orlando, FL-Nov. 2011 – Present
   ◆ Planned workshops and events to foster the professional growth of the members in my organization
   ◆ Recognized as most professional, most likely to become CEO, and most likely to succeed
   ◆ Raised over $1,500 in 7 weeks as my pledge class's Vice President of Fundraising
Sales Club *Member*
Society for Marketing Professional Services (SMPS) *Member*

Professional Experience

Enterprise Rent-A- Car - *Management Training Program Intern*   Orlando, FL- Mar. 2012 – Present
   ◆ Gaining a vast experience in customer service, marketing and management within a sales environment
   ◆ Acquiring a strong communication, interpersonal and leadership skills by helping run multi-million dollar business
Tutor Matching Service - *Director of Campus Operations*   Orlando, FL-Aug. 2011 - Present
   ◆ Responsible for recruitment, training and management of the UCF Tutor Matching Service team
   ◆ Develop and execute presentations to UCF department heads , which concluded in a strategic partnership with SGA
   ◆ Build and maintain relationships with organizations at UCF, which lead to an increase of 70 tutors
Universal Studios - *Sales Assistant/Vendor*   Orlando, FL-Mar. 2007 - Present
   ◆ Recognized as the top vendor in my department in sales and customer service
   ◆ Utilized several up-selling and cross-selling sales techniques to consistently meet the quota
   ◆ Cross trained in all aspects of the merchandise department
Salesgravy.com - *Sales Intern*   Orlando, FL- Aug. 2011 – Dec.2011
   ◆ Cold called over 75 different companies and maintained a closing rate of 8.7%
   ◆ Utilized and built a comprehensive database using a CRM Program to improve customer satisfaction

Other Experience

Revenue Performance	Account Manager Intern	Jan.2011-May 2011
Publix Super Market	Deli Clerk	Aug. 2010- Mar. 2011
Galaxy Vacations	Sales Associate/Tour guide	May 2008- Aug. 2011
Vector Marketing	Sales Associate	Jan. 2010 - Apr. 2010
Protostar International	Intern	Jan. 2009 - May 2009
International Financing Consultant	Intern	May 2008- Aug. 2010

Community Service

YMCA   Orlando, FL
   ◆ Coached soccer at the Dr. Phillips YMCA for four seasons resulting in over 150 community service hours
American Cancer Society   Orlando, FL
   ◆ Participated in fundraiser which generated over $20,000 and 75 hours of community service
Boystown of Central Florida   Oviedo, FL
   ◆ Advocated fundraising concepts with four teammates and coordinated efforts to raise over $3500 in one semester

To: Frito-Lay Company North America

Re: **Mr. Daniel Botero**

Date: April 9, 2012

As both a former Frito-Lay National Brand Manager Brand Manager-Dallas/Plano, TX (Doritos® Brand Tortilla Chips, Ruffles® Brand Potato chips, Lay's® Brand Potato Chips) and as a collegiate instructor quite familiar with Mr. Daniel Botero, I am most pleased to highly recommend him for a career position with Frito-Lay North America for the following key reasons:

- **Mr. Botero knows the "power of the shelf" and is constantly driven to excel over any and all competition.**
- **Mr. Botero is eager to enter the world of grocery supply where he can work effectively with major consumer brands while successfully managing and partnering with the critical retail supply chain.**
- **Mr. Botero possesses a very sound personal character and exemplifies outstanding leadership values & qualities in all of his work.**
- **Mr. Botero has a growing experience background in the general business world that provides him with very practical judgment capabilities.**
- **Mr. Botero has an excellent record of campus and civic related activities and achievements.**
- **Mr. Botero also brings a valuable bilingual skill to Frito-Lay's operations in the Florida market.**
- **Mr. Botero well understands and employs the model of *servant leadership.***

Should you require any additional information concerning Mr. Botero, please contact me at my University of Central Florida campus office. (407) 823-5974.

Sincerely yours,

Karl Sooder,
Instructor/ Marketing

After The Interview

Just because the interview is over, it does not mean your job is over. You still need to make sure you are following up and staying top of mind. You want to make sure that you follow-up right away. You need to make sure that as soon as you can get in front of your computer that you are sending the person who interviewed you an email to thank them and follow-up. In this email you want to thank

182

them again for the opportunity to interview and reiterate why you think you are a good fit for the role and how you will help solve a problem that they have. The second thing I want you to make sure that you do is to write them a hand-written thank you note. Send it in the mail as soon as you can. Another option is to write the hand-written card in the lobby or waiting area and hand it to the receptionist before you leave. Many times, you will not be the only candidate interviewing that day so making sure you stay top of mind is crucial. What happens most of the time is that they conduct interviews all day and at the end of the day they will collaborate and determine who moves forward and who does not. Anything that you can do to stay top of mind will help increase your chances of being selected. This is why it's important to send the email as soon as possible. Most people have email on their phone and will check in between interviews. When they check their email and see that you followed up so quickly it will make a difference.

CONCLUSION

CHAPTER 17
RECAP THE 3 A'S

I am so excited that you have made it to the end of the book! It shows a whole other level of commitment to your future. It is said that knowledge is power, but that's not exactly true. Taking action on that knowledge is power. Actually implementing and executing what you have learned is power. By reading this book you have armed yourself with the tools that you need to land your dream job. Now, all that's left is to execute what you've learned using those tools. Promise yourself that you will take action so that you can make your dreams a reality! In this final chapter, I will recap some of the biggest takeaways from the book to help you land your dream job before graduation. The program consists of the three A's: Assess, Acquire, and Achieve.

Assess

After reading this section you should understand why self-discovery is so important. Taking the time now to complete self-assessments will save you time, money, and energy in the long term. It is crucial that you complete the exercises provided in this section. If you skipped it and told yourself that you will come back to it later, you are making a big mistake. Take action and do it now! There's a good chance that you will get busy and never come back to it. It is crucial to complete the self-assessment before implementing everything else that we've covered in the book. Every section builds on the previous one and I've put the sections in this order for a reason.

Acquire

In this section, we picked up exactly where we left off with Assess. You learned that landing your dream job is like acing an open book test. There should be no surprises as to what each company looks for in their ideal candidates as long as you take the time to do the research. I explained the 10-5-1 activity which I truly believe will be one of the most important things you do to get the answers to your open book test and build relationships. We talked about how being strategic with your time is a must and how there are many different ways to build the skills needed to become the ideal candidate. You now know that networking is king and that more than 80% of jobs are filled through referrals. You also know my personal networking strategy which will help you to build long lasting, mutually beneficial relationships. You should now think of yourself as a million-dollar-brand because you are! Run yourself like a business in order to be the best version of yourself. Finally, we finished this section talking about all the benefits that you have because you are a student.. and there are a lot! Make sure that you take full advantage of all of these benefits. The goal of this section is to show you all of the different resources available that you can use to position yourself as the ideal candidate. This is the longest step of the program so don't get discouraged! It takes time, but I know you can do it!

Achieve

The goal of this section is to help you cross the finish line and land your dream job before you graduate. We started off this section discussing how to stand out among the crowd. This is necessary in order for you to land your dream job, or any job at all for that matter. Create personalized marketing materials like business cards, thank you cards, a website, and a portfolio. We talked a lot about LinkedIn.This is the most important social media platform for students especially because your profile will be viewed more than your resume. You should now know how to create an all-star LinkedIn profile and how to create content that allows you to build great relationships with employers before you even meet them in person. I explained how to master the career fair and walk away with interviews. We went over resumes and I explained why this piece of paper is the most biased document in the world. We also covered the importance of handing your resume to the right person. This practically guarantees your resume will be reviewed in detail and not get dismissed by an ATS or a six-second recruiter scan. All of this leads to you landing an interview. We covered what you should do before the interview, during the interview, and after the interview.

CHAPTER 18
CONCLUSION

Finding Your Dream Job Is Like Finding Your Soulmate

The best analogy that I can think of to compare finding your dream job to is finding your soulmate. In the beginning, you will probably feel uncomfortable or awkward about dating and meeting someone new. You may lack confidence and think that because you have no experience that no one is going to want to talk to you. Little by little, you will start figuring it out and things will start making sense. You will start experimenting to try and figure out what your type is and what is not. This is similar to the start of building your professional career. You are looking for a new job and you have no idea where to start. You will start exploring to figure out what job you will like the most. You become a little bit more selective in what you are looking for in your "significant other." This comes from personal experience or from seeing others experience it. You may start taking classes in your major and realize that major is not for you. Or, you may work at a theme park one summer and fall in love with the atmosphere and change your major to hospitality. The possibilities are endless, but you get the point. Everyday that goes by you gather more and more information that allows you to keep narrowing your search. Then you finally meet someone and it feels like love at first sight. Similarly, you could learn about an opportunity with a company and feel like it was love at first sight. In real life, a love at first sight experience does not happen for everyone and it's the same when it comes to looking for a job. Maybe your soulmate ends up being your friend from high school who you knew all along, but never considered him/her in that way. This too can happen with your dream job. You end up working for the company your uncle has been working at for the past twenty years. You never thought much of it, but when you gave them a chance they were the perfect match.

Similar to marriage, you go through multiple steps before committing. Students should not just rush to say yes the first time they meet the employer. You need to do as much as possible to get to know them better. You can accomplish this by doing an internship, externship, or maybe even spending a day in the office to get a better idea of what a typical day looks like. You also go through the interview process, in which you should be interviewing them too. All of this should be to allow both you and the company to make the best mutual decision.

When selecting your soulmate company I want you to make sure you see yourself with them for at least two years. It doesn't have to be for life like you would hope for in a marriage, but it should be at least for two years. This will give you time to gain enough experience from your first job and at the same time will be worth the investment for the company that gave you a shot.

Final Thoughts

From the bottom of my heart, I thank you for investing your time, money, and energy into reading this book. My goal for writing this book was to give you the blueprint on how to master college and land your dream job before graduation. I promise that if you follow what you learn from this book that you will not be part of the 67% of students who graduate college without a job. I promise that you will not only have a job, but it will be a job that you love.

I recently listened to a podcast where the guest said that focus is more important than knowledge. I think this is so true. While writing this book, I thought back about the hundreds of students who I have personally helped and how they have been able to reach their goals. I've realized that what they all had in common was focus. With focus, you can gain knowledge. If you think back on what you learned throughout this book you will see that focus is a common theme. You can do anything, but you can't do everything.

Do you remember Danielle and Mike from the example in the beginning of the book?

A week after speaking with Mike's professor, I got an email from Mike and it said, "Hi Daniel, Professor Johnson shared that you would be interested in speaking to me about a job after college…." I replied back and said, "Mike, I personally don't have a job to offer for you, but I help students like you find their dream job. I would be more than happy to set up a time for us to talk and help you develop a game plan." Needless to say, I never heard back from Mike. This is not uncommon as some students don't want to do the work that it takes. Last I heard, Mike is still at the same job he had before he graduated and other than being a college graduate, not much has changed for him. On the other hand, Danielle had a very different outcome. I ended up working with Danielle and teaching her what you have learned in this book. I am not going to lie, it was not all smooth sailing. You have to remember she called me less than a month before graduation. But ultimately, she was able to get a job as a sales associate with PepsiCo three months after graduation. Since she started with PepsiCo, she has gotten married and has even been promoted to district sales leader.

Now the rest is up to you! You have a decision to make. You can hope that you will get a great job just by graduating or you can follow the advice given in this book that has helped hundreds of students walk across the graduation stage with their dream job!

I truly hope you choose to take advantage of the three-step program explained in this book. Your first job out of college will set the foundation for the rest of your professional life. If you choose to follow this program, then you just gained an ally. It is now in my best interest to make sure you graduate with your dream job. If you get stuck at any point in this process and want my advice email me at Daniel@MasteringCollegeToCareer.Com and I will reply. I also want to know about your successes. If you apply anything you learn in this book and find success I ask that you let me know and do me a favor by buying someone starting college a copy of this book. Together we can impact millions of students' lives!

CONGRATULATIONS ON FINISHING THE BOOK!

You should be proud you made it to the end of the book. The reality is that most people don't get this far.

This means you are serious about your career and I want to reward that.

I have one more video for you!

Or Visit:
http://bit.ly/masteringcollegelastvideo

Sources

Fact: 67% of college students graduate without a job lined up*

Source: Student Voices

Link: https://mystudentvoices.com/collegegradjobs-e581bdc078d2

Location in Book: Chapter one

Fact: 40% of graduates are in jobs that don't require a degree**

Source: Th Washington Post

Link:https://www.washingtonpost.com/news/grade-point/wp/2018/09/01/college-students-say-they-want-a-degree-for-a-job-are-they-getting-what-they-want/?noredirect=on&utm_term=.eaba89085da3

Location in Book: Chapter one

Fact: The average college student is taking six years to graduate with a four-year degree***

Source: National Center for Education Statistics

Link: https://nces.ed.gov/fastfacts/display.asp?id=569

Location in Book: Chapter 1

Fact: On average students are graduating with $30,000 in student debt****

Source: CNBC

Link:https://www.cnbc.com/2019/05/20/how-much-the-average-student-loan-borrower-owes-when-they-graduate.html

Location in Book: Chapter 1

Fact: According to a study by the Society for Human Resources Management (SHRM), it could cost up to five times a bad hire's annual salary.

Source: SHRM

Link: https://insights.dice.com/report/the-cost-of-bad-hiring-decisions/

Location in Book: Chapter 6

Fact: According to Forbes, 91% of college seniors thought they had the skills to get the job they wanted, but 98% of recruiters said they get resumes from applicants who are not qualified for the position

Source: Forbes

Link:https://www.forbes.com/sites/nickmorrison/2017/04/23/the-class-of-2017-face-a-reality-check-when-they-graduate-college/#632f1f083b56

Location in Book Chapter 6

Fact: Within 3 years of initial enrollment, about 30 percent of undergraduates in associate's and bachelor's degree programs who had declared a major had changed their major at least once

Source: U.S Department of Education

Link: https://nces.ed.gov/pubs2018/2018434.pdf

Location in Book: Chapter 8

Fact: It is said that over 85% of jobs are filled through networking

Source: LinkedIn

Link:https://www.linkedin.com/pulse/new-survey-reveals-85-all-jobs-filled-via-networking-lou-adler/

Location in Book: Chapter 9

Fact: Salesforce is the #2 company to work for 2019

Source: Great place to work

Link:https://www.greatplacetowork.com/best-workplaces/100-best/2019

Location in Book: Chapter 9

Fact: On average students are graduating with $30,000 in student debt****

Source: CNBC

Link:https://www.cnbc.com/2019/05/20/how-much-the-average-student-loan-borrower-owes-when-they-graduate.html

Location in Book: Chapter 10

SUBSCRIBE TO THE PODCAST!

If you like the book, you will love the podcast
https://linktr.ee/masteringcollegetocareer

URGENT PLEA!

Thank You For Reading My Book!

I really appreciate all of your feedback, and I love hearing what you have to say.

I need your input to make the next version of this book and my future books better.

Please leave me a helpful review on Amazon letting me know what you thought of the book.

Thanks so much!!

- Daniel Botero

Made in the USA
Middletown, DE
13 November 2019

78543198R00117